CANDIDA • SHAW, GEORGE BERNARD

Publisher's Note

Purchase of this book entitles you to a free trial membership in the publisher's book club at www.rarebooksclub.com. (Time limited offer.) Simply enter the barcode number from the back cover onto the membership form on our home page. The book club entitles you to select from millions of books at no additional charge. You can also download a digital copy of this and related books to read on the go. Simply enter the title or subject onto the search form to find them.

Note: This is an historic book. Pages numbers, where present in the text, refer to the first edition of the book and may also be in indexes.

If you have any questions, could you please be so kind as to consult our Frequently Asked Questions page at www.rarebooksclub.com/faqs.cfm? You are also welcome to contact us there.
Publisher: General Books LLC™, Memphis, TN, USA, 2012. ISBN: 9781153594035.
Proofreading: pgdp.net

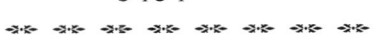

CANDIDA

BERNARD SHAW

1898

ACT I 1

ACT II 10

ACT III 17

ACT I

A fine October morning in the north east suburbs of London, a vast district many miles away from the London of Mayfair and St. James's, much less known there than the Paris of the Rue de Rivoli and the Champs Elysees, and much less narrow, squalid, fetid and airless in its slums; strong in comfortable, prosperous middle class life; wide-streeted, myriad-populated; well-served with ugly iron urinals, Radical clubs, tram lines, and a perpetual stream of yellow cars; enjoying in its main thoroughfares the luxury of grass-grown "front gardens," untrodden by the foot of man save as to the path from the gate to the hall door; but blighted by an intolerable monotony of miles and miles of graceless, characterless brick houses, black iron railings, stony pavements, slaty roofs, and respectably ill dressed or disreputably poorly dressed people, quite accustomed to the place, and mostly plodding about somebody else's work, which they would not do if they themselves could help it. The little energy and eagerness that crop up show themselves in cockney cupidity and business "push." Even the policemen and the chapels are not infrequent enough to break the monotony. The sun is shining cheerfully; there is no fog; and though the smoke effectually prevents anything, whether faces and hands or bricks and mortar, from looking fresh and clean, it is not hanging heavily enough to trouble a Londoner.

This desert of unattractiveness has its oasis. Near the outer end of the Hackney Road is a park of 217 acres, fenced in, not by railings, but by a wooden paling, and containing plenty of greensward, trees, a lake for bathers, flower beds with the flowers arranged carefully in patterns by the admired cockney art of carpet gardening and a sandpit, imported from the seaside for the delight of the children, but speedily deserted on its becoming a natural vermin preserve for all the petty fauna of Kingsland, Hackney and Hoxton. A bandstand, an unfinished forum for religious, anti-religious and political orators, cricket pitches, a gymnasium, and an old fashioned stone kiosk are among its attractions. Wherever the prospect is bounded by trees or rising green grounds, it is a pleasant place. Where the ground stretches far to the grey palings, with bricks and mortar, sky signs, crowded chimneys and smoke beyond, the prospect makes it desolate and sordid.

The best view of Victoria Park is from the front window of St. Dominic's Parsonage, from which not a single chimney is visible. The parsonage is a semi-detached villa with a front garden and a porch. Visitors go up the flight of steps to the porch: tradespeople and members of the family go down by a door under the steps to the basement, with a breakfast room, used for all meals, in front, and the kitchen at the back. Upstairs, on the level of the hall door, is the drawing-room, with its large plate glass window looking on the park. In this room, the only sitting-room that can be spared from the children and the family meals, the parson, the Reverend James Mavor Morell does his work. He is sitting in a strong round backed revolving chair at the right hand end of a long table, which stands across the window, so that he can cheer himself with the view of the park at his elbow. At the opposite end of the table, adjoining it, is a little table; only half the width of the other, with a typewriter on it. His typist is sitting at this machine, with her back to the window. The large table is littered with pamphlets, journals, letters, nests of drawers, an office diary, postage scales and the like. A spare chair for visitors having business with the person is in the middle, turned to his end. Within reach of his hand is a stationery case, and a cabinet photograph in a frame. Behind him the right hand wall, recessed above the fireplace, is fitted with bookshelves, on which an adept eye can measure the parson's divinity and casuistry by a complete set of Browning's poems and Maurice's Theological Essays, and guess at his politics from a yellow backed Progress and Poverty, Fabian Essays, a Dream of John Ball, Marx's Capital, and half a dozen other literary landmarks in Socialism. Opposite him on the left, near the typewriter, is the door. Further down the room, opposite the fireplace, a bookcase stands on a cellaret, with a sofa near it. There is a generous fire burning; and the hearth, with a comfortable armchair and a japanned flower painted coal scuttle at one side, a miniature chair for a boy or girl on the other, a nicely varnished wooden mantelpiece, with neatly moulded shelves, tiny bits of mirror let into the panels, and a travelling clock in a leather case (the inevitable wedding present), and on the wall above a large autotype of the chief figure in Titian's Virgin of the Assumption, is very inviting. Altogether the room is the room of a good housekeeper, vanquished, as far as the table is concerned, by an untidy man, but elsewhere mistress of the situation. The furniture, in its ornamental aspect, betrays the style of the advertised "drawing-room suite" of the pushing suburban furniture dealer; but there is nothing useless or pretentious in the room. The paper and panelling are dark, throwing the big cheery window and the park outside into strong relief.

The Reverend James Mavor Morell is a Christian Socialist clergyman of the Church of England, and an active member of the Guild of St. Matthew and the Christian Social Union. A vigorous, genial, popular man of forty, robust and goodlooking, full of energy, with pleasant, hearty, considerate manners, and a sound, unaffected voice, which he uses with the clean, athletic articulation of a practised orator, and with a wide range and perfect command of expression. He is a first rate clergyman, able to say what he likes to whom he likes, to lecture people without setting himself up against them, to impose his authority on them without humiliating them, and to interfere in their business without impertinence. His well-spring of spiritual enthusiasm and sympathetic emotion has never run dry for a moment: he still eats and sleeps heartily enough to win the daily battle between exhaustion and recuperation triumphantly. Withal, a great baby, pardonably vain of his powers and unconsciously pleased with himself. He has a healthy complexion, a good forehead, with the brows somewhat blunt, and the eyes bright and eager, a mouth resolute, but not particularly well cut, and a substantial nose, with the mobile, spreading nostrils of the dramatic orator, but, like all his features, void of subtlety.

The typist, Miss Proserpine Garnett, is a brisk little woman of about 30, of the lower middle class, neatly but cheaply dressed in a black merino skirt and a blouse, rather pert and quick of speech, and not very civil in her manner, but sensitive and affectionate. She is clattering away busily at her machine whilst Morell opens the last of his morning's letters. He realizes its contents with a comic groan of despair.

PROSERPINE. Another lecture?

MORELL. Yes. The Hoxton Freedom Group want me to address them on Sunday morning (great emphasis on "Sunday," this being the unreasonable part of the business). What are they?

PROSERPINE. Communist Anarchists, I think.

MORELL. Just like Anarchists not to know that they can't have a parson on Sunday! Tell them to come to church if they want to hear me: it will do them good. Say I can only come on Mondays and Thursdays. Have you the diary there?

PROSERPINE (taking up the diary). Yes.

MORELL. Have I any lecture on for next Monday?

PROSERPINE (referring to diary). Tower Hamlets Radical Club.

MORELL. Well, Thursday then?

PROSERPINE. English Land Restoration League.

MORELL. What next?

PROSERPINE. Guild of St. Matthew on Monday. Independent Labor Party, Greenwich Branch, on Thursday. Monday, Social-Democratic Federation, Mile End Branch. Thursday, first Confirmation class— (Impatiently). Oh, I'd better tell them you can't come. They're only half a dozen ignorant and conceited costermongers without five shillings between them.

MORELL (amused). Ah; but you see they're near relatives of mine, Miss Garnett.

PROSERPINE (staring at him). Relatives of YOURS!

MORELL. Yes: we have the same father—in Heaven.

PROSERPINE (relieved). Oh, is that all?

MORELL (with a sadness which is a luxury to a man whose voice expresses it so finely). Ah, you don't believe it. Everybody says it: nobody believes it—nobody. (Briskly, getting back to business.) Well, well! Come, Miss Proserpine, can't you find a date for the costers? What about the 25th?: that was vacant the day before yesterday.

PROSERPINE (referring to diary). Engaged—the Fabian Society.

MORELL. Bother the Fabian Society! Is the 28th gone too?

PROSERPINE. City dinner. You're invited to dine with the Founder's Company.

MORELL. That'll do; I'll go to the Hoxton Group of Freedom instead. (She enters the engagement in silence, with implacable disparagement of the Hoxton Anarchists in every line of her face. Morell bursts open the cover of a copy of The Church Reformer, which has come by post, and glances through Mr. Stewart Hendlam's leader and the Guild of St. Matthew news. These proceedings are presently enlivened by the appearance of Morell's curate, the Reverend Alexander Mill, a young gentleman gathered by Morell from the nearest University settlement, whither he had come from Oxford to give the east end of London the benefit of his university training. He is a conceitedly well intentioned, enthusiastic, immature person, with nothing positively unbearable about him except a habit of speaking with his lips carefully closed for half an inch from each corner, a finicking arthulation, and a set of horribly corrupt vowels, notably ow for o, this being his chief means of bringing Oxford refinement to bear on Hackney vulgarity.

Morell, whom he has won over by a doglike devotion, looks up indulgently from The Church Reformer as he enters, and remarks) Well, Lexy! Late again, as usual.

LEXY. I'm afraid so. I wish I could get up in the morning.

MORELL (exulting in his own energy). Ha! ha! (Whimsically.) Watch and pray, Lexy: watch and pray.

LEXY. I know. (Rising wittily to the occasion.) But how can I watch and pray when I am asleep? Isn't that so, Miss Prossy?

PROSERPINE (sharply). Miss Garnett, if you please.

LEXY. I beg your pardon—Miss Garnett.

PROSERPINE. You've got to do all the work to-day.

LEXY. Why?

PROSERPINE. Never mind why. It will do you good to earn your supper before you eat it, for once in a way, as I do. Come: don't dawdle. You should have been off on your rounds half an hour ago.

LEXY (perplexed). Is she in earnest, Morell?

MORELL (in the highest spirits—his eyes dancing). Yes. *I* am going to dawdle to-day.

LEXY. You! You don't know how.

MORELL (heartily). Ha! ha! Don't I? I'm going to have this day all to myself—or at least the forenoon. My wife's coming back: she's due here at 11.45.

LEXY (surprised). Coming back already—with the children? I thought they were to stay to the end of the month.

MORELL. So they are: she's only coming up for two days, to get some flannel things for Jimmy, and to see how we're getting on without her.

LEXY (anxiously). But, my dear Morell, if what Jimmy and Fluffy had was scarlatina, do you think it wise—

MORELL. Scarlatina!—rubbish, German measles. I brought it into the house myself from the Pycroft Street School. A parson is like a doctor, my boy: he must face infection as a soldier must face bullets. (He rises and claps Lexy on the shoulder.) Catch the measles if you can, Lexy: she'll nurse you; and what a piece of luck that will be for you!—eh?

LEXY (smiling uneasily). It's so hard to understand you about Mrs. Morell—

MORELL (tenderly). Ah, my boy, get married—get married to a good woman; and then you'll understand. That's a foretaste of what will be best in the Kingdom of Heaven we are trying to establish on earth. That will cure you of dawdling. An honest man feels that he must pay Heaven for every hour of happiness with a good spell of hard, unselfish work to make others happy. We have no more right to consume happiness without producing it than to consume wealth without producing it. Get a wife like my Candida; and you'll always be in arrear with your repayment. (He pats Lexy affectionately on the back, and is leaving the room when Lexy calls to him.)

LEXY. Oh, wait a bit: I forgot. (Morell halts and turns with the door knob in his hand.) Your father-in-law is coming round to see you. (Morell shuts the door again, with a complete change of manner.)

MORELL (surprised and not pleased). Mr. Burgess?

LEXY. Yes. I passed him in the park, arguing with somebody. He gave me good day and asked me to let you know that he was coming.

MORELL (half incredulous). But he hasn't called here for—I may almost say for years. Are you sure, Lexy? You're not joking, are you?

LEXY (earnestly). No, sir, really.

MORELL (thoughtfully). Hm! Time for him to take another look at Candida before she grows out of his knowledge. (He resigns himself to the inevitable, and goes out. Lexy looks after him with beaming, foolish worship.)

LEXY. What a good man! What a thorough, loving soul he is! (He takes Morell's place at the table, making himself very comfortable as he takes out a cigaret.)

PROSERPINE (impatiently, pulling the letter she has been working at off the typewriter and folding it.) Oh, a man ought to be able to be fond of his wife without making a fool of himself about her.

LEXY (shocked). Oh, Miss Prossy!

PROSERPINE (rising busily and coming to the stationery case to get an envelope, in which she encloses the letter as she speaks). Candida here, and Candida there, and Candida everywhere! (She licks the envelope.) It's enough to drive anyone out of their SENSES (thumping the envelope to make it stick) to hear a perfectly commonplace woman raved about in that absurd manner merely because she's got good hair, and a tolerable figure.

LEXY (with reproachful gravity). I think her extremely beautiful, Miss Garnett. (He takes the photograph up; looks at it; and adds, with even greater impressiveness) EXTREMELY beautiful. How fine her eyes are!

PROSERPINE. Her eyes are not a bit better than mine—now! (He puts down the photograph and stares austerely at her.) And you know very well that you think me dowdy and second rate enough.

LEXY (rising majestically). Heaven forbid that I should think of any of God's creatures in such a way! (He moves stiffly away from her across the room to the neighbourhood of the bookcase.)

PROSERPINE. Thank you. That's very nice and comforting.

LEXY (saddened by her depravity). I had no idea you had any feeling against Mrs. Morell.

PROSERPINE (indignantly). I have no feeling against her. She's very nice, very good-hearted: I'm very fond of her and can appreciate her real qualities far better than any man can. (He shakes his head sadly and turns to the bookcase, looking along the shelves for a volume. She follows him with intense pepperiness.) You don't believe me? (He turns and faces her. She pounces at him with spitfire energy.) You think I'm jealous. Oh, what a profound knowledge of the human heart you have, Mr. Lexy Mill! How well you know the weaknesses of Woman, don't you? It must be so nice to be a man and have a fine penetrating intellect instead of mere emotions like us, and to know that the reason we don't share your amorous delusions is that we're all jealous of one another! (She abandons him with a toss of her shoulders, and crosses to the fire to warm her hands.)

LEXY. Ah, if you women only had the same clue to Man's strength that you have to his weakness, Miss Prossy, there would be no Woman Question.

PROSERPINE (over her shoulder, as she stoops, holding her hands to the blaze). Where did you hear Morell say that? You didn't invent it yourself: you're not clever enough.

LEXY. That's quite true. I am not ashamed of owing him that, as I owe him so many other spiritual truths. He said it at the annual conference of the Women's Liberal Federation. Allow me to add that though they didn't appreciate it, I, a mere man, did. (He turns to the bookcase again, hoping that this may leave her crushed.)

PROSERPINE (putting her hair straight at the little panel of mirror in the mantelpiece). Well, when you talk to me, give me your own ideas, such as they are, and not his. You never cut a poorer figure than when you are trying to imitate him.

LEXY (stung). I try to follow his example, not to imitate him.

PROSERPINE (coming at him again on her way back to her work). Yes, you do: you IMITATE him. Why do you tuck your umbrella under your left arm instead of carrying it in your hand like anyone else? Why do you walk with your chin stuck out before you, hurrying along with that eager look in your eyes—you, who never get up before half past nine in the morning? Why do you say "knoaledge" in church, though you always say "knollege" in private conversation! Bah! do you think I don't know? (She goes back to the typewriter.) Here, come and set about your work: we've wasted enough time for one morning. Here's a copy of the diary for to-day. (She hands him a memorandum.)

LEXY (deeply offended). Thank you. (He takes it and stands at the table with his back to her, reading it. She begins to transcribe her shorthand notes on the typewriter without troubling herself about his feelings. Mr. Burgess enters unannounced. He is a man of sixty, made coarse and sordid by the compulsory selfishness of petty commerce, and later on softened into sluggish bumptiousness by overfeeding and commercial success. A vulgar, ignorant, guzzling man, offensive and contemptuous to people whose labor is cheap, respectful to wealth and rank, and quite sincere and without rancour or envy in both attitudes. Finding him without talent, the world has offered him no decently paid work except ignoble work, and he has become in consequence, somewhat hoggish. But he has no suspicion of this himself, and honestly regards his commercial prosperity as the inevitable and socially wholesome triumph of the ability, industry, shrewdness and experience in business of a man who in private is easygoing, affectionate and humorously convivial to a fault. Corporeally, he is a podgy man, with a square, clean shaven face and a square beard under his chin; dust colored, with a patch of grey in the centre, and small watery blue eyes with a plaintively sentimental expression, which he transfers easily to his voice by his habit of pompously intoning his sentences.)

BURGESS (stopping on the threshold, and looking round). They told me Mr. Morell was here.

PROSERPINE (rising). He's upstairs. I'll fetch him for you.

BURGESS (staring boorishly at her). You're not the same young lady as used to typewrite for him?

PROSERPINE. No.

BURGESS (assenting). No: she was younger. (Miss Garnett stolidly stares at him; then goes out with great dignity. He receives this quite obtusely, and crosses to the hearth-rug, where he turns and spreads himself with his back to the fire.) Startin' on your rounds, Mr. Mill?

LEXY (folding his paper and pocketing it). Yes: I must be off presently.

BURGESS (momentously). Don't let me detain you, Mr. Mill. What I come about is private between me and Mr. Morell.

LEXY (huffily). I have no intention of intruding, I am sure, Mr. Burgess. Good morning.

BURGESS (patronizingly). Oh, good morning to you. (Morell returns as Lexy is making for the door.)

MORELL (to Lexy). Off to work?

LEXY. Yes, sir.

MORELL (patting him affectionately on the shoulder). Take my silk handkerchief and wrap your throat up. There's a cold wind. Away with you.

(Lexy brightens up, and goes out.)

BURGESS. Spoilin' your curates, as usu'l, James. Good mornin'. When I pay a man, an' 'is livin' depen's on me, I keep him in his place.

MORELL (rather shortly). I always keep my curates in their places as my helpers and comrades. If you get as much work out of your clerks and warehousemen as I do out of my curates, you must be getting rich pretty fast. Will you take your old chair?

(He points with curt authority to the arm chair beside the fireplace; then takes the spare chair from the table and sits down in front of Burgess.)

BURGESS (without moving). Just the same as hever, James!

MORELL. When you last called—it was about three years ago, I think—you said the same thing a little more frankly. Your exact words then were: "Just as big a fool as ever, James?"

BURGESS (soothingly). Well, perhaps I did; but (with conciliatory cheerfulness) I meant no offence by it. A clergyman is privileged to be a bit of a fool, you know: it's on'y becomin' in his profession that he should. Anyhow, I come here, not to rake up hold differences, but to let bygones be bygones. (Suddenly becoming very solemn, and approaching Morell.) James: three year ago, you done me a hill turn. You done me hout of a contrac'; an' when I gev you 'arsh words in my nat'ral disappointment, you turned my daughter again me. Well, I've come to act the part of a Cherischin. (Offering his hand.) I forgive you, James.

MORELL (starting up). Confound your impudence!

BURGESS (retreating, with almost lachrymose deprecation of this treatment). Is that becomin' language for a clergyman, James?—and you so partic'lar, too?

MORELL (hotly). No, sir, it is not becoming language for a clergyman. I used the wrong word. I should have said damn your impudence: that's what St. Paul, or any honest priest would have said to you. Do you think I have forgotten that tender of yours for the contract to supply clothing to the workhouse?

BURGESS (in a paroxysm of public spirit). I acted in the interest of the ratepayers, James. It was the lowest tender: you can't deny that.

MORELL. Yes, the lowest, because you paid worse wages than any other employer—starvation wages—aye, worse than starvation wages—to the women who made the clothing. Your wages would have driven them to the streets to keep body and soul together. (Getting angrier and angrier.) Those women were my parishioners. I shamed the Guardians out of accepting your tender: I shamed the ratepayers out of letting them do it: I shamed everybody but you. (Boiling over.) How dare you, sir, come here and offer to forgive me, and talk about your daughter, and—

BURGESS. Easy, James, easy, easy. Don't git hinto a fluster about nothink. I've howned I was wrong.

MORELL (fuming about). Have you? I didn't hear you.

BURGESS. Of course I did. I hown it now. Come: I harsk your pardon for the letter I wrote you. Is that enough?

MORELL (snapping his fingers). That's nothing. Have you raised the wages?

BURGESS (triumphantly). Yes.

MORELL (stopping dead). What!

BURGESS (unctuously). I've turned a moddle hemployer. I don't hemploy no women now: they're all sacked; and the work is done by machinery. Not a man 'as less than sixpence a hour; and the skilled 'ands gits the Trade Union rate. (Proudly.) What 'ave you to say to me now?

MORELL (overwhelmed). Is it possible! Well, there's more joy in heaven over one sinner that repenteth— (Going to Burgess with an explosion of apologetic cordiality.) My dear Burgess, I most heartily beg your pardon for my hard thoughts of you. (Grasps his hand.) And now, don't you feel the better for the change? Come, confess, you're happier. You look happier.

BURGESS (ruefully). Well, p'raps I do. I s'pose I must, since you notice it. At all events, I git my contrax asseppit (accepted) by the County Council. (Savagely.) They dussent'ave nothink to do with me unless I paid fair wages—curse 'em for a parcel o' meddlin' fools!

MORELL (dropping his hand, utterly discouraged). So that was why you raised the wages! (He sits down moodily.)

BURGESS (severely, in spreading, mounting tones). Why else should I do it? What does it lead to but drink and huppishness in workin' men? (He seats himself magisterially in the easy chair.) It's hall very well for you, James: it gits you hinto the papers and makes a great man of you; but you never think of the 'arm you do, puttin' money into the pockets of workin' men that they don't know 'ow to spend, and takin' it from people that might be makin' a good huse on it.

MORELL (with a heavy sigh, speaking with cold politeness). What is your business with me this morning? I shall not pretend to believe that you are here merely out of family sentiment.

BURGESS (obstinately). Yes, I ham—just family sentiment and nothink else.

MORELL (with weary calm). I don't believe you!

BURGESS (rising threateningly). Don't say that to me again, James Mavor Morell.

MORELL (unmoved). I'll say it just as often as may be necessary to convince you that it's true. I don't believe you.

BURGESS (collapsing into an abyss of wounded feeling). Oh, well, if you're determined to be unfriendly, I s'pose I'd better go. (He moves reluctantly towards the door. Morell makes no sign. He lingers.) I didn't hexpect to find a hunforgivin' spirit in you, James. (Morell still not responding, he takes a few more reluctant steps doorwards. Then he comes back whining.) We huseter git on well enough, spite of our different opinions. Why are you so changed to me? I give you my word I come here in pyorr (pure) frenl'ness, not wishin' to be on bad terms with my hown daughrter's 'usban'. Come, James: be a Cherishin and shake 'ands. (He puts his hand sentimentally on Morell's shoulder.)

MORELL (looking up at him thoughtfully). Look here, Burgess. Do you want to be as welcome here as you were before you lost that contract?

BURGESS. I do, James. I do—honest.

MORELL. Then why don't you behave as you did then?

BURGESS (cautiously removing his hand). 'Ow d'y'mean?

MORELL. I'll tell you. You thought me a young fool then.

BURGESS (coaxingly). No, I d dn't, James. I—

MORELL (cutting him short). Yes, you did. And I thought you an old scoundrel.

BURGESS (most vehemently deprecating this gross self-accusation on Morell's part). No, you didn't, James. Now you do yourself a hinjustice.

MORELL. Yes, I did. Well, that did not prevent our getting on very well together. God made you what I call a scoundrel as he made me what you call a fool (The effect of this observation on Burgess is to remove the keystone of his moral arch. He becomes bodily weak, and, with his eyes fixed on Morell in a helpless stare, puts out his hand apprehensively to balance himself, as if the floor had suddenly sloped under him. Morell proceeds in the same tone of quiet conviction.) It was not for me to quarrel with his handiwork in the one case more than in the other. So long as you come here honestly as a self-respecting, thorough, convinced scoundrel, justifying your scoundrelism, and proud of it, you are welcome. But (and now Morell's tone becomes formidable and he rises and strikes the back of the chair for greater emphasis) I won't have you here snivelling about being a model employer and a converted man when you're only an apostate with your coat turned for the sake of a County Council contract. (He nods at him to enforce the point; then goes to the hearth-rug, where he takes up a comfortably commanding position with his back to the fire, and continues) No: I like a man to be true to himself, even in wickedness. Come now: either take your hat and go; or else sit down and give me a good scoundrelly reason for wanting to be friends with me. (Burgess, whose emotions have subsided sufficiently to be expressed by a dazed grin, is relieved by this concrete proposition. He ponders it for a moment, and then, slowly and very modestly, sits down in the chair Morell has just left.) That's right. Now, out with it.

BURGESS (chuckling in spite of himself.) Well, you ARE a queer bird, James, and no mistake. But (almost enthusiastically) one carnt 'elp likin' you; besides, as I said afore, of course one don't take all a clorgyman says seriously, or the world couldn't go on. Could it now? (He composes himself for graver discourse, and turning his eyes on Morell proceeds with dull seriousness.) Well, I don't mind tellin' you, since it's your wish we should be free with one another, that I did think you a bit of a fool once; but I'm beginnin' to think that p'r'aps I was be'ind the times a bit.

MORELL (delighted). Aha! You're finding that out at last, are you?

BURGESS (portentously). Yes, times 'as changed mor'n I could a believed. Five yorr (year) ago, no sensible man would a thought o' takin' up with your ideas. I hused to wonder you was let preach at all. Why, I know a clorgyman that 'as bin kep' hout of his job for yorrs by the Bishop of London, although the pore feller's not a bit more religious than you are. But to-day, if henyone was to offer to bet me a thousan' poun' that you'll end by bein' a bishop yourself, I shouldn't venture to take the bet. You and yore crew are gettin' hinfluential: I can see that. They'll 'ave to give you something someday, if it's only to stop yore mouth. You 'ad the right instinc' arter all, James: the line you took is the payin' line in the long run fur a man o' your sort.

MORELL (decisively—offering his hand). Shake hands, Burgess. Now you're talking honestly. I don't think they'll make me a bishop; but if they do, I'll introduce you to the biggest jobbers I can get to come to my dinner parties.

BURGESS (who has risen with a sheepish grin and accepted the hand of friendship). You will 'ave your joke, James. Our quarrel's made up now, isn't it?

A WOMAN'S VOICE. Say yes, James.

Startled, they turn quickly and find that Candida has just come in, and is looking at them with an amused maternal indulgence which is her characteristic expression. She is a woman of 33, well built, well nourished, likely, one guesses, to become matronly later on, but now quite at her best, with the double charm of youth and motherhood. Her ways are those of a woman who has found that she can always manage people by engaging their affection, and who does so frankly and instinctively without the smallest scruple. So far, she is like any other pretty woman who is just clever enough to make the most of her sexual attractions for trivially selfish ends; but Candida's serene brow, courageous eyes, and well set mouth and chin signify largeness of mind and dignity of character to ennoble her cunning in the affections. A wisehearted observer, looking at her, would at once guess that whoever had placed the Virgin of the Assumption over her hearth did so because he fancied some spiritual resemblance between them, and yet would not suspect either her husband or herself of any such idea, or indeed of any concern with the art of Titian.

Just now she is in bonnet and mantle, laden with a strapped rug with her umbrella stuck through it, a handbag, and a supply of illustrated papers.

MORELL (shocked at his remissness). Candida! Why—(looks at his watch, and is horrified to find it so late.) My darling! (Hurrying to her and seizing the rug strap, pouring forth his remorseful regrets all the time.) I intended to meet you at the train. I let the time slip. (Flinging the rug on the sofa.) I was so engrossed by—(returning to her)—I forgot—oh! (He embraces her with penitent emotion.)

BURGESS (a little shamefaced and doubtful of his reception). How ors you, Candy? (She, still in Morell's arms, offers him her cheek, which he kisses.) James and me is come to a unnerstandin'—a honourable unnerstandin'. Ain' we, James?

MORELL (impetuously). Oh, bother your understanding! You've kept me late for Candida. (With compassionate fervor.) My poor love: how did you manage about the luggage?—how—

CANDIDA (stopping him and disengaging herself). There, there, there. I wasn't alone. Eugene came down yesterday; and we traveled up together.

MORELL (pleased). Eugene!

CANDIDA. Yes: he's struggling with my luggage, poor boy. Go out, dear, at once; or he will pay for the cab; and I don't want that. (Morell hurries out. Candida puts down her handbag; then takes off her mantle and bonnet and puts them on the sofa with the rug, chatting meanwhile.) Well, papa, how are you getting on at home?

BURGESS. The 'ouse ain't worth livin' in since you left it, Candy. I wish you'd come round and give the gurl a talkin' to. Who's this Eugene that's come with you?

CANDIDA. Oh, Eugene's one of James's discoveries. He found him sleeping on the Embankment last June. Haven't you noticed our new picture (pointing to the Virgin)? He gave us that.

BURGESS (incredulously). Garn! D'you mean to tell me—your hown father!—that cab touts or such like, orf the Embankment, buys pictur's like that? (Severely.) Don't deceive me, Candy: it's a 'Igh Church pictur; and James chose it hisself.

CANDIDA. Guess again. Eugene isn't a cab tout.

BURGESS. Then wot is he? (Sarcastically.) A nobleman, I 'spose.

CANDIDA (delighted—nodding). Yes. His uncle's a peer—a real live earl.

BURGESS (not daring to believe such good news). No!

CANDIDA. Yes. He had a seven day bill for 55 pounds in his pocket when James found him on the Embankment. He thought he couldn't get any money for it until the seven days were up; and he was too shy to ask for credit. Oh, he's a dear boy! We are very fond of him.

BURGESS (pretending to belittle the aristocracy, but with his eyes gleaming). Hm, I thort you wouldn't git a piorr's (peer's) nevvy visitin' in Victoria Park unless he were a bit of a flat. (Looking again at the picture.) Of course I don't 'old with that pictur, Candy; but still it's a 'igh class, fust rate work of art: I can see that. Be sure you hintroduce me to him, Candy. (He looks at his watch anxiously.) I can only stay about two minutes.

Morell comes back with Eugene, whom Burgess contemplates moist-eyed with enthusiasm. He is a strange, shy youth of eighteen, slight, effeminate, with a delicate childish voice, and a hunted, tormented expression and shrinking manner that show the painful sensitiveness that very swift and acute apprehensiveness produces in youth, before the character has grown to its full strength. Yet everything that his timidity and frailty suggests is contradicted by his face. He is miserably irresolute, does not know where to stand or what to do with his hands and feet, is afraid of Burgess, and would run away into solitude if he dared; but the very intensity with which he feels a perfectly commonplace position shows great nervous force, and his nostrils and mouth show a fiercely petulant wilfulness, as to the quality of which his great imaginative eyes and fine brow are reassuring. He is so entirely uncommon as to be almost unearthly; and to prosaic people there is something noxious in this unearthliness, just as to poetic people there is something angelic in it. His dress is anarchic. He wears an old blue serge jacket, unbuttoned over a woollen lawn tennis shirt, with a silk handkerchief for a cravat, trousers matching the jacket, and brown canvas shoes. In these garments he has apparently lain in the heather and waded through the waters; but there is no evidence of his having ever brushed them.

As he catches sight of a stranger on entering, he stops, and edges along the wall on the opposite side of the room.

MORELL (as he enters). Come along: you can spare us quarter of an hour, at all events. This is my father-in-law, Mr. Burgess—Mr. Marchbanks.

MARCHBANKS (nervously backing against the bookcase). Glad to meet you, sir.

BURGESS (crossing to him with great heartiness, whilst Morell joins Candida at the fire). Glad to meet YOU, I'm shore, Mr. Morchbanks. (Forcing him to shake hands.) 'Ow do you find yoreself this weather? 'Ope you ain't lettin' James put no foolish ideas into your 'ed?

MARCHBANKS. Foolish ideas! Oh, you mean Socialism. No.

BURGESS. That's right. (Again looking at his watch.) Well, I must go now: there's no 'elp for it. Yo're not comin' my way, are you, Mr. Morchbanks?

MARCHBANKS. Which way is that?

BURGESS. Victawriar Pork station. There's a city train at 12.25.

MORELL. Nonsense. Eugene will stay to lunch with us, I expect.

MARCHBANKS (anxiously excusing himself). No—I—I—

BURGESS. Well, well, I shan't press you: I bet you'd rather lunch with Candy. Some night, I 'ope, you'll come and dine with me at my club, the Freeman Founders in Nortn Folgit. Come, say you will.

MARCHBANKS. Thank you, Mr. Burgess. Where is Norton Folgate—down in Surrey, isn't it? (Burgess, inexpressibly tickled, begins to splutter with laughter.)

CANDIDA (coming to the rescue). You'll lose your train, papa, if you don't go at once. Come back in the afternoon and tell Mr. Marchbanks where to find the club.

BURGESS (roaring with glee). Down in Surrey—har, har! that's not a bad one. Well, I never met a man as didn't know Nortn Folgit before. (Abashed at his own noisiness.) Goodbye, Mr. Morchbanks: I know yo're too 'ighbred to take my pleasantry in bad part. (He again offers his hand.)

MARCHBANKS (taking it with a nervous jerk). Not at all.

BURGESS. Bye, bye, Candy. I'll look in again later on. So long, James.

MORELL. Must you go?

BURGESS. Don't stir. (He goes out with unabated heartiness.)

MORELL. Oh, I'll see you out. (He follows him out. Eugene stares after them apprehensively, holding his breath until Burgess disappears.)

CANDIDA (laughing). Well, Eugene. (He turns with a start and comes eagerly towards her, but stops irresolutely as he meets her amused look.) What do you think of my father?

MARCHBANKS. I—I hardly know him yet. He seems to be a very nice old gentleman.

CANDIDA (with gentle irony). And you'l go to the Freeman Founders to dine with him, won't you?

MARCHBANKS (miserably, taking it quite seriously). Yes, if it will please you.

CANDIDA (touched). Do you know, you are a very nice boy, Eugene, with all your queerness. If you had laughed at my father I shouldn't have minded; but I like you ever so much better for being nice to him.

MARCHBANKS. Ought I to have laughed? I noticed that he said something funny; but I am so ill at ease with strangers; and I never can see a joke! I'm very sorry. (He sits down on the sofa, his elbows on his knees and his temples between his fists, with an expression of hopeless suffering.)

CANDIDA (bustling him goodnaturedly). Oh, come! You great baby, you! You are worse than usual this morning. Why were you so melancholy as we came along in the cab?

MARCHBANKS. Oh, that was nothing. I was wondering how much I ought to give the cabman. I know it's utterly silly; but you don't know how dreadful such things are to me—how I shrink from having to deal with strange people. (Quickly and reassuringly.) But it's all right. He beamed all over and touched his hat when Morell gave him two shillings. I was on the point of offering him ten. (Candida laughs heartily. Morell comes back with a few letters and newspapers which have come by the midday post.)

CANDIDA. Oh, James, dear, he was going to give the cabman ten shillings—ten shillings for a three minutes' drive—oh, dear!

MORELL (at the table, glancing through the letters). Never mind her, Marchbanks. The overpaying instinct is a generous one: better than the underpaying instinct, and not so common.

MARCHBANKS (relapsing into dejection). No: cowardice, incompetence. Mrs. Morell's quite right.

CANDIDA. Of course she is. (She takes up her handbag.) And now I must leave you to James for the present. I suppose you are too much of a poet to know the state a woman finds her house in when she's been away for three weeks. Give me my rug. (Eugene takes the strapped rug from the couch, and gives it to her. She takes it in her left hand, having the bag in her right.) Now hang my cloak across my arm. (He obeys.) Now my hat. (He puts it into the hand which has the bag.) Now open the door for me. (He hurries up before her and opens the door.) Thanks. (She goes out; and Marchbanks shuts the door.)

MORELL (still busy at the table). You'll stay to lunch, Marchbanks, of course.

MARCHBANKS (scared). I mustn't. (He glances quickly at Morell, but at once avoids his frank look, and adds, with obvious disingenuousness) I can't.

MORELL (over his shoulder). You mean you won't.

MARCHBANKS (earnestly). No: I should like to, indeed. Thank you very much. But—but—

MORELL (breezily, finishing with the letters and coming close to him). But—but—but—but—bosh! If you'd like to stay, stay. You don't mean to persuade me you have anything else to do. If you're shy, go and take a turn in the park and write poetry until half past one; and then come in and have a good feed.

MARCHBANKS. Thank you, I should like that very much. But I really mustn't. The truth is, Mrs. Morell told me not to. She said she didn't think you'd ask me to stay to lunch, but that I was to remember, if you did, that you didn't really want me to. (Plaintively.) She said I'd understand; but I don't. Please don't tell her I told you.

MORELL (drolly). Oh, is that all? Won't my suggestion that you should take a turn in the park meet the difficulty?

MARCHBANKS. How?

MORELL (exploding good-humoredly). Why, you duffer—(But this boisterousness jars himself as well as Eugene. He checks himself, and resumes, with affectionate seriousness) No: I won't put it in that way. My dear lad: in a happy marriage like ours, there is something very sacred in the return of the wife to her home. (Marchbanks looks quickly at him, half anticipating his meaning.) An old friend or a truly noble and sympathetic soul is not in the way on such occasions; but a chance visitor is. (The hunted, horror-stricken expression comes out with sudden vividness in Eugene's face as he understands. Morell, occupied with his own thought, goes on without noticing it.) Candida thought I would rather not have you here; but she was wrong. I'm very fond of you, my boy, and I should like you to see for yourself what a happy thing it is to be married as I am.

MARCHBANKS. Happy!—YOUR marriage! You think that! You believe that!

MORELL (buoyantly). I know it, my lad. La Rochefoucauld said that there are convenient marriages, but no delightful ones. You don't know the comfort of seeing through and through a thundering liar and rotten cynic like that fellow. Ha, ha! Now off with you to the park, and write your poem. Half past one, sharp, mind: we never wait for anybody.

MARCHBANKS (wildly). No: stop: you shan't. I'll force it into the light.

MORELL (puzzled). Eh? Force what?

MARCHBANKS. I must speak to you. There is something that must be settled between us.

MORELL (with a whimsical glance at the clock). Now?

MARCHBANKS (passionately). Now. Before you leave this room. (He retreats a few steps, and stands as if to bar Morell's way to the door.)

MORELL (without moving, and gravely, perceiving now that there is something serious the matter). I'm not going to leave it, my dear boy: I thought YOU were. (Eugene, baffled by his firm tone, turns his back on him, writhing with anger. Morell goes to him and puts his hand on his shoulder strongly and kindly, disregarding his attempt to shake it off) Come: sit down quietly; and tell me what it is. And remember; we are friends, and need not fear that either of us will be anything but patient and kind to the other, whatever we may have to say.

MARCHBANKS (twisting himself round on him). Oh, I am not forgetting myself: I am only (covering his face desperately with his hands) full of horror. (Then, dropping his hands, and thrusting his face forward fiercely at Morell, he goes on threateningly.) You shall see whether this is a time for patience and kindness. (Morell, firm as a rock, looks indulgently at him.) Don't look at me in that self-complacent way. You think yourself stronger than I am; but I shall stagger you if you have a heart in your breast.

MORELL (powerfully confident). Stagger me, my boy. Out with it.

MARCHBANKS. First—

MORELL. First?

MARCHBANKS. I love your wife.

(Morell recoils, and, after staring at him for a moment in utter amazement, bursts into uncontrollable laughter. Eugene is taken aback, but not disconcerted; and he soon becomes indignant and contemptuous.)

MORELL (sitting down to have his laugh out). Why, my dear child, of course you do. Everybody loves her: they can't help it. I like it. But (looking up whimsically at him) I say, Eugene: do you think yours is a case to be talked about? You're under twenty: she's over thirty. Doesn't it look rather too like a case of calf love?

MARCHBANKS (vehemently). YOU dare say that of her! You think that way of the love she inspires! It is an insult to her!

MORELL (rising; quickly, in an altered tone). To her! Eugene: take care. I have been patient. I hope to remain patient. But there are some things I won't allow. Don't force me to show you the indulgence I should show to a child. Be a man.

MARCHBANKS (with a gesture as if sweeping something behind him). Oh, let us put aside all that cant. It horrifies me when I think of the doses of it she has had to endure in all the weary years during which you have selfishly and blindly sacrificed her to minister to your self-sufficiency—YOU (turning on him) who have not one thought—one sense—in common with her.

MORELL (philosophically). She seems to bear it pretty well. (Looking him straight in the face.) Eugene, my boy: you are making a fool of yourself—a very great fool of yourself. There's a piece of wholesome plain speaking for you.

MARCHBANKS. Oh, do you think I don't know all that? Do you think that the things people make fools of themselves about are any less real and true than the things they behave sensibly about? (Morell's gaze wavers for the first time. He instinctively averts his face and stands listening, startled and thoughtful.) They are more true: they are the only things that are true. You are very calm and sensible and moderate with me because you can see that I am a fool about your wife; just as no doubt that old man who was here just now is very wise over your socialism, because he sees that YOU are a fool about it. (Morell's perplexity deepens markedly. Eugene follows up his advantage, plying him fiercely with questions.) Does that prove you wrong? Does your complacent superiority to me prove that I am wrong?

MORELL (turning on Eugene, who stands his ground). Marchbanks: some devil is putting these words into your mouth. It is easy—terribly easy—to shake a man's faith in himself. To take advantage of that to break a man's spirit is devil's work. Take care of what you are doing. Take care.

MARCHBANKS (ruthlessly). I know. I'm doing it on purpose. I told you I should stagger you.

(They confront one another threateningly for a moment. Then Morell recovers his dignity.)

MORELL (with noble tenderness). Eugene: listen to me. Some day, I hope and trust, you will be a happy man like me. (Eugene chafes intolerantly, repudiating the worth of his happiness. Morell, deeply insulted, controls himself with fine forbearance, and continues steadily, with great artistic beauty of delivery) You will be married; and you will be working with all your might and valor to make every spot on earth as happy as your own home. You will be one of the makers of the Kingdom of Heaven on earth; and—who knows?—you may be a pioneer and master builder where I am only a humble journeyman; for don't think, my boy, that I cannot see in you, young as you are, promise of higher powers than I can ever pretend to. I well know that it is in the poet that the holy spirit of man—the god within him—is most godlike. It should make you tremble to think of that—to think that the heavy burthen and great gift of a poet may be laid upon you.

MARCHBANKS (unimpressed and remorseless, his boyish crudity of assertion telling sharply against Morell's oratory). It does not make me tremble. It is the want of it in others that makes me tremble.

MORELL (redoubling his force of style under the stimulus of his genuine feeling and Eugene's obduracy). Then help to kindle it in them—in ME—-not to extinguish it. In the future—when you are as happy as I am—I will be your true brother in the faith. I will help you to believe that God has given us a world that nothing but our own folly keeps from being a paradise. I will help you to believe that every stroke of your work is sowing happiness for the great harvest that all—even the humblest—shall one day reap. And last, but trust me, not least, I will help you to believe that your wife loves you and is happy in her home. We need such help, Marchbanks: we need it greatly and always. There are so many things to make us doubt, if once we let our understanding be troubled. Even at home, we sit as if in camp, encompassed by a hostile army of doubts. Will you play the traitor and let them in on me?

MARCHBANKS (looking round him). Is it like this for her here always? A woman, with a great soul, craving for reality, truth, freedom, and being fed on metaphors, sermons, stale perorations, mere rhetoric. Do you think a woman's soul can live on your talent for preaching?

MORELL (Stung). Marchbanks: you make it hard for me to control myself. My talent is like yours insofar as it has any real worth at all. It is the gift of finding words for divine truth.

MARCHBANKS (impetuously). It's the gift of the gab, nothing more and nothing less. What has your knack of fine talking to do with the truth, any more than playing the organ has? I've never been in your church; but I've been to your political meetings; and I've seen you do what's called rousing the meeting to enthusiasm: that is, you excited them until they behaved exactly as if they were drunk. And their wives looked on and saw clearly enough what fools they were. Oh, it's an old story: you'll find it in the Bible. I imagine King David, in his fits of enthusiasm, was very like you. (Stabbing him with the words.) "But his wife despised him in her heart."

MORELL (wrathfully). Leave my house Do you hear? (He advances on him threateningly.)

MARCHBANKS (shrinking back against the couch). Let me alone. Don't touch me. (Morell grasps him powerfully by the lapel of his coat: he cowers down on the sofa and screams passionately.) Stop, Morell, if you strike me, I'll kill myself. I won't bear it. (Almost in hysterics.) Let me go. Take your hand away.

MORELL (with slow, emphatic scorn.) You little snivelling, cowardly whelp. (Releasing him.) Go, before you frighten yourself into a fit.

MARCHBANKS (on the sofa, gasping, but relieved by the withdrawal of Morell's hand). I'm not afraid of you: it's you who are afraid of me.

MORELL (quietly, as he stands over him). It looks like it, doesn't it?

MARCHBANKS (with petulant vehemence). Yes, it does. (Morell turns away contemptuously. Eugene scrambles to his feet and follows him.) You think because I shrink from being brutally handled—because (with tears in his voice) I can do nothing but cry with rage when I am met with violence—because I can't lift a heavy trunk down from the top of a cab like you—because I can't fight you for your wife as a navvy would: all that makes you think that I'm afraid of you. But you're wrong. If I haven't got what you call British pluck, I haven't British cowardice either: I'm not afraid of a clergyman's ideas. I'll fight your ideas. I'll rescue her from her slavery to them: I'll pit my own ideas against them. You are driving me out of the house because you daren't let her choose between your ideas and mine. You are afraid to let me see her again. (Morell, angered, turns suddenly on him. He flies to the door in involuntary dread.) Let me alone, I say. I'm going.

MORELL (with cold scorn). Wait a moment: I am not going to touch you: don't be afraid. When my wife comes back she will want to know why you have gone. And when she finds that you are never going to cross our threshold again, she will want to have that explained, too. Now I don't wish to distress her by telling her that you have behaved like a blackguard.

MARCHBANKS (Coming back with renewed vehemence). You shall—you must. If you give any explanation but the true one, you are a liar and a coward. Tell her what I said; and how you were strong and manly, and shook me as a terrier shakes a rat; and how I shrank and was terrified; and how you called me a snivelling little whelp and put me out of the house. If you don't tell her, I will: I'll write to her.

MORELL (taken aback.) Why do you want her to know this?

MARCHBANKS (with lyric rapture.) Because she will understand me, and know that I understand her. If you keep back one word of it from her—if you are not ready to lay the truth at her feet as I am—then you will know to the end of your days that she really belongs to me and not to you. Good-bye. (Going.)

MORELL (terribly disquieted). Stop: I will not tell her.

MARCHBANKS (turning near the door). Either the truth or a lie you MUST tell her, if I go.

MORELL (temporizing). Marchbanks: it is sometimes justifiable.

MARCHBANKS (cutting him short). I know—to lie. It will be useless. Good-bye, Mr. Clergyman.

(As he turns finally to the door, it opens and Candida enters in housekeeping attire.)

CANDIDA. Are you going, Eugene?(Looking more observantly at him.) Well, dear me, just look at you, going out into the street in that state! You ARE a poet, certainly. Look at him, James! (She takes him by the coat, and brings him forward to show him to Morell.) Look at his collar! look at his tie! look at his hair! One would think somebody had been throttling you. (The two men guard themselves against betraying their consciousness.) Here! Stand still. (She buttons his collar; ties his neckerchief in a bow; and arranges his hair.) There! Now you look so nice that I think you'd better stay to lunch after all, though I told you you mustn't. It will be ready in half an hour. (She puts a final touch to the bow. He kisses her hand.) Don't be silly.

MARCHBANKS. I want to stay, of course—unless the reverend gentleman, your husband, has anything to advance to the contrary.

CANDIDA. Shall he stay, James, if he promises to be a good boy and to help me to lay the table? (Marchbanks turns his head and looks steadfastly at Morell over his shoulder, challenging his answer.)

MORELL (shortly). Oh, yes, certainly: he had better. (He goes to the table and pretends to busy himself with his papers there.)

MARCHBANKS (offering his arm to Candida). Come and lay the table.(She takes it and they go to the door together. As they go out he adds) I am the happiest of men.

MORELL. So was I—an hour ago.

ACT II

The same day. The same room. Late in the afternoon. The spare chair for visitors has been replaced at the table, which is, if possible, more untidy than before. Marchbanks, alone and idle, is trying to find out how the typewriter works. Hearing someone at the door, he steals guiltily away to the window and pretends to be absorbed in the view. Miss Garnett, carrying the notebook in which she takes down Morell's letters in shorthand from his dictation, sits down at the typewriter and sets to work transcribing them, much too busy to notice Eugene. Unfortunately the first key she strikes sticks.

PROSERPINE. Bother! You've been meddling with my typewriter, Mr. Marchbanks; and there's not the least use in your trying to look as if you hadn't.

MARCHBANKS (timidly). I'm very sorry, Miss Garnett. I only tried to make it write.

PROSERPINE. Well, you've made this key stick.

MARCHBANKS (earnestly). I assure you I didn't touch the keys. I didn't, indeed. I only turned a little wheel. (He points irresolutely at the tension wheel.)

PROSERPINE. Oh, now I understand. (She sets the machine to rights, talking volubly all the time.) I suppose you thought it was a sort of barrel-organ. Nothing to do but turn the handle, and it would write a beautiful love letter for you straight off, eh?

MARCHBANKS (seriously). I suppose a machine could be made to write love-letters. They're all the same, aren't they!

PROSERPINE (somewhat indignantly: any such discussion, except by way of pleasantry, being outside her code of manners). How do I know? Why do you ask me?

MARCHBANKS. I beg your pardon. I thought clever people—people who can do business and write letters, and that sort of thing—always had love affairs.

PROSERPINE (rising, outraged). Mr. Marchbanks! (She looks severely at him, and marches with much dignity to the bookcase.)

MARCHBANKS (approaching her humbly). I hope I haven't offended you. Perhaps I shouldn't have alluded to your love affairs.

PROSERPINE (plucking a blue book from the shelf and turning sharply on him). I haven't any love affairs. How dare you say such a thing?

MARCHBANKS (simply). Really! Oh, then you are shy, like me. Isn't that so?

PROSERPINE. Certainly I am not shy. What do you mean?

MARCHBANKS (secretly). You must be: that is the reason there are so few love affairs in the world. We all go about longing for love: it is the first need of our natures, the loudest cry Of our hearts; but we dare not utter our longing: we are too shy. (Very earnestly.) Oh, Miss Garnett, what would you not give to be without fear, without shame—

PROSERPINE (scandalized), Well, upon my word!

MARCHBANKS (with petulant impatience). Ah, don't say those stupid things to me: they don't deceive me: what use are they? Why are you afraid to be your real self with me? I am just like you.

PROSERPINE. Like me! Pray, are you flattering me or flattering yourself? I don't feel quite sure which. (She turns to go back to the typewriter.)

MARCHBANKS (stopping her mysteriously). Hush! I go about in search of love; and I find it in unmeasured stores in the bosoms of others. But when I try to ask for it, this horrible shyness strangles me; and I stand dumb, or worse than dumb, saying meaningless things—foolish lies. And I see the affection I am longing for given to dogs and cats and pet birds, because they come and ask for it. (Almost whispering.) It must be asked for: it is like a ghost: it cannot speak unless it is first spoken to. (At his normal pitch, but with deep melancholy.) All the love in the world is longing to speak; only it dare not, because it is shy, shy, shy. That is the world's tragedy. (With a deep sigh he sits in the spare chair and buries his face in his hands.)

PROSERPINE (amazed, but keeping her wits about her—her point of honor in encounters with strange young men). Wicked people get over that shyness occasionally, don't they?

MARCHBANKS (scrambling up almost fiercely). Wicked people means people who have no love: therefore they have no shame. They have the power to ask love because they don't need it: they have the power to offer it because they have none to give. (He collapses into his seat, and adds, mournfully) But we, who have love, and long to mingle it with the love of others: we cannot utter a word. (Timidly.) You find that, don't you?

PROSERPINE. Look here: if you don't stop talking like this, I'll leave the room, Mr. Marchbanks: I really will. It's not proper. (She resumes her seat at the typewriter, opening the blue book and preparing to copy a passage from it.)

MARCHBANKS (hopelessly). Nothing that's worth saying IS proper. (He rises, and wanders about the room in his lost way, saying) I can't understand you, Miss Garnett. What am I to talk about?

PROSERPINE (snubbing him). Talk about indifferent things, talk about the weather.

MARCHBANKS. Would you stand and talk about indifferent things if a child were by, crying bitterly with hunger?

PROSERPINE. I suppose not.

MARCHBANKS. Well: I can't talk about indifferent things with my heart crying out bitterly in ITS hunger.

PROSERPINE. Then hold your tongue.

MARCHBANKS. Yes: that is what it always comes to. We hold our tongues. Does that stop the cry of your heart?—for it does cry: doesn't it? It must, if you have a heart.

PROSERPINE (suddenly rising with her hand pressed on her heart). Oh, it's no use trying to work while you talk like that. (She leaves her little table and sits on the sofa. Her feelings are evidently strongly worked on.) It's no business of yours, whether my heart cries or not; but I have a mind to tell you, for all that.

MARCHBANKS. You needn't. I know already that it must.

PROSERPINE. But mind: if you ever say I said so, I'll deny it.

MARCHBANKS (compassionately). Yes, I know. And so you haven't the courage to tell him?

PROSERPINE (bouncing up). HIM! Who?

MARCHBANKS. Whoever he is. The man you love. It might be anybody. The curate, Mr. Mill, perhaps.

PROSERPINE (with disdain). Mr. Mill!!! A fine man to break my heart about, indeed! I'd rather have you than Mr. Mill.

MARCHBANKS (recoiling). No, really—I'm very sorry; but you mustn't think of that. I—

PROSERPINE. (testily, crossing to the fire and standing at it with her back to him). Oh, don't be frightened: it's not you. It's not any one particular person.

MARCHBANKS. I know. You feel that you could love anybody that offered—

PROSERPINE (exasperated). Anybody that offered! No, I do not. What do you take me for?

MARCHBANKS (discouraged). No use. You won't make me REAL answers—only those things that everybody says. (He strays to the sofa and sits down disconsolately.)

PROSERPINE (nettled at what she takes to be a disparagement of her manners by an aristocrat). Oh, well, if you want original conversation, you'd better go and talk to yourself.

MARCHBANKS. That is what all poets do: they talk to themselves out loud; and the world overhears them. But it's horribly lonely not to hear someone else talk sometimes.

PROSERPINE. Wait until Mr. Morell comes. HE'LL talk to you. (Marchbanks shudders.) Oh, you needn't make wry faces over him: he can talk better than you. (With temper.) He'd talk your little head off. (She is going back angrily to her place, when, suddenly enlightened, he springs up and stops her.)

MARCHBANKS. Ah, I understand now!

PROSERPINE (reddening). What do you understand?

MARCHBANKS. Your secret. Tell me: is it really and truly possible for a woman to love him?

PROSERPINE (as if this were beyond all bounds). Well!!

MARCHBANKS (passionately). No, answer me. I want to know: I MUST know. I can't understand it. I can see nothing in him but words, pious resolutions, what people call goodness. You can't love that.

PROSERPINE (attempting to snub him by an air of cool propriety). I simply don't know what you're talking about. I don't understand you.

MARCHBANKS (vehemently). You do. You lie—

PROSERPINE. Oh!

MARCHBANKS. You DO understand; and you KNOW. (Determined to have an answer.) Is it possible for a woman to love him?

PROSERPINE (looking him straight in the face.) Yes. (He covers his face with his hands.) Whatever is the matter with you! (He takes down his hands and looks at her. Frightened at the tragic mask presented to her, she hurries past him at the utmost possible distance, keeping her eyes on his face until he turns from her and goes to the child's chair beside the hearth, where he sits in the deepest dejection. As she approaches the door, it opens and Burgess enters. On seeing him, she ejaculates) Praise heaven, here's somebody! (and sits down, reassured, at her table. She puts a fresh sheet of paper into the typewriter as Burgess crosses to Eugene.)

BURGESS (bent on taking care of the distinguished visitor). Well: so this is the way they leave you to yourself, Mr. Morchbanks. I've come to keep you company. (Marchbanks looks up at him in consternation, which is quite lost on him.) James is receivin' a deppitation in the dinin' room; and Candy is hupstairs educatin' of a young stitcher gurl she's hinterusted in. She's settin' there learnin' her to read out of the "'Ev'nly Twins." (Condolingly.) You must find it lonesome here with no one but the typist to talk to. (He pulls round the easy chair above fire, and sits down.)

PROSERPINE (highly incensed). He'll be all right now that he has the advantage of YOUR polished conversation: that's one comfort, anyhow. (She begins to typewrite with clattering asperity.)

BURGESS (amazed at her audacity). Hi was not addressin' myself to you, young woman, that I'm awerr of.

PROSERPINE (tartly, to Marchbanks). Did you ever see worse manners, Mr. Marchbanks?

BURGESS (with pompous severity). Mr. Morchbanks is a gentleman and knows his place, which is more than some people do.

PROSERPINE (fretfully). It's well you and I are not ladies and gentlemen: I'd talk to you pretty straight if Mr. Marchbanks wasn't here. (She pulls the letter out of the machine so crossly that it tears.) There, now I've spoiled this letter—have to be done all over again. Oh, I can't contain myself—silly old fathead!

BURGESS (rising, breathless with indignation). Ho! I'm a silly ole fathead, am I? Ho, indeed (gasping). Hall right, my gurl! Hall right. You just wait till I tell that to your employer. You'll see. I'll teach you: see if I don't.

PROSERPINE. I—

BURGESS (cutting her short). No, you've done it now. No huse a-talkin' to me. I'll let you know who I am. (Proserpine shifts her paper carriage with a defiant bang, and disdainfully goes on with her work.) Don't you take no notice of her, Mr. Morchbanks. She's beneath it. (He sits down again loftily.)

MARCHBANKS (miserably nervous and disconcerted). Hadn't we better change the subject. I—I don't think Miss Garnett meant anything.

PROSERPINE (with intense conviction). Oh, didn't I though, just!

BURGESS. I wouldn't demean myself to take notice on her.

(An electric bell rings twice.)

PROSERPINE (gathering up her notbook and papers). That's for me. (She hurries out.)

BURGESS (calling after her). Oh, we can spare you. (Somewhat relieved by the triumph of having the last word, and yet half inclined to try to improve on it, he looks after her for a moment; then subsides into his seat by Eugene, and addresses him very confidentially.) Now we're alone, Mr. Morchbanks, let me give you a friendly 'int that I wouldn't give to everybody. 'Ow long 'ave you known my son-in-law James here?

MARCHBANKS. I don't know. I never can remember dates. A few months, perhaps.

BURGESS. Ever notice anything queer about him?

MARCHBANKS. I don't think so.

BURGESS (impressively). No more you wouldn't. That's the danger in it. Well, he's mad.

MARCHBANKS. Mad!

BURGESS. Mad as a Morch 'are. You take notice on him and you'll see.

MARCHBANKS (beginning). But surely that is only because his opinions—

BURGESS (touching him with his forefinger on his knee, and pressing it as if to hold his attention with it). That's wot I used tee think, Mr. Morchbanks. Hi thought long enough that it was honly 'is hopinions; though, mind you, hopinions becomes vurry serious things when people takes to hactin on 'em as 'e does. But that's not wot I go on. (He looks round to make sure that they are alone, and bends over to Eugene's ear.

) Wot do you think he says to me this mornin' in this very room?

MARCHBANKS. What?

BURGESS. He sez to me—this is as sure as we're settin' here now—he sez: "I'm a fool," he sez;—"and yore a scounderl"—as cool as possible. Me a scounderl, mind you! And then shook 'ands with me on it, as if it was to my credit! Do you mean to tell me that that man's sane?

MORELL. (outside, calling to Proserpine, holding the door open). Get all their names and addresses, Miss Garnett.

PROSERPINE (in the distance). Yes, Mr. Morell.

(Morell comes in, with the deputation's documents in his hands.)

BURGESS (aside to Marchbanks). Yorr he is. Just you keep your heye on him and see. (Rising momentously.) I'm sorry, James, to 'ave to make a complaint to you. I don't want to do it; but I feel I oughter, as a matter o' right and duty.

MORELL. What's the matter?

BURGESS. Mr. Morchbanks will bear me out: he was a witness. (Very solemnly.) Your young woman so far forgot herself as to call me a silly ole fat 'ead.

MORELL (delighted—with tremendous heartiness). Oh, now, isn't that EXACTLY like Prossy? She's so frank: she can't contain herself! Poor Prossy! Ha! Ha!

BURGESS (trembling with rage). And do you hexpec me to put up with it from the like of 'ER?

MORELL. Pooh, nonsense! you can't take any notice of it. Never mind. (He goes to the cellaret and puts the papers into one of the drawers.)

BURGESS. Oh, I don't mind. I'm above it. But is it RIGHT?—that's what I want to know. Is it right?

MORELL. That's a question for the Church, not for the laity. Has it done you any harm, that's the question for you, eh? Of course, it hasn't. Think no more of it. (He dismisses the subject by going to his place at the table and setting to work at his correspondence.)

BURGESS (aside to Marchbanks). What did I tell you? Mad as a 'atter. (He goes to the table and asks, with the sickly civility of a hungry man) When's dinner, James?

MORELL. Not for half an hour yet.

BURGESS (with plaintive resignation). Gimme a nice book to read over the fire, will you, James: thur's a good chap.

MORELL. What sort of book? A good one?

BURGESS (with almost a yell of remonstrance). Nah-oo! Summat pleasant, just to pass the time. (Morell takes an illustrated paper from the table and offers it. He accepts it humbly.) Thank yer, James. (He goes back to his easy chair at the fire, and sits there at his ease, reading.)

MORELL (as he writes). Candida will come to entertain you presently. She has got rid of her pupil. She is filling the lamps.

MARCHBANKS (starting up in the wildest consternation). But that will soil her hands. I can't bear that, Morell: it's a shame. I'll go and fill them. (He makes for the door.)

MORELL. You'd better not. (Marchbanks stops irresolutely.) She'd only set you to clean my boots, to save me the trouble of doing it myself in the morning.

BURGESS (with grave disapproval) Don't you keep a servant now, James?

MORELL. Yes; but she isn't a slave: and the house looks as if I kept three That means that everyone has to lend a hand. It's not a bad plan: Prossy and I can talk business after breakfast whilst we're washing up. Washing up's no trouble when there are two people to do it.

MARCHBANKS (tormentedly). Do you think every woman is as coarse-grained as Miss Garnett?

BURGESS (emphatically). That's quite right, Mr. Morchbanks. That's quite right. She IS corse-grained.

MORELL (quietly and significantly). Marchbanks!

MARCHBANKS. Yes.

MORELL. How many servants does your father keep?

MARCHBANKS. Oh, I don't know.

(He comes back uneasily to the sofa, as if to get as far as possible from Morell's questioning, and sits down in great agony of mind, thinking of the paraffin.)

MORELL. (very gravely). So many that you don't know. (More aggressively.) Anyhow, when there's anything coarse-grained to be done, you ring the bell and throw it on to somebody else, eh? That's one of the great facts in YOUR existence, isn't it?

MARCHBANKS. Oh, don't torture me. The one great fact now is that your wife's beautiful fingers are dabbling in paraffin oil, and that you are sitting here comfortably preaching about it—everlasting preaching, preaching, words, words, words.

BURGESS (intensely appreciating this retort). Ha, ha! Devil a better. (Radiantly.) 'Ad you there, James, straight.

(Candida comes in, well aproned, with a reading lamp trimmed, filled, and ready for lighting. She places it on the table near Morell, ready for use.)

CANDIDA (brushing her finger tips together with a slight twitch of her nose). If you stay with us, Eugene, I think I will hand over the lamps to you.

MARCHBANKS. I will stay on condition that you hand over all the rough work to me.

CANDIDA. That's very gallant, but I think I should like to see how you do it first. (Turning to Morell.) James: you've not been looking after the house properly.

MORELL. What have I done—or not done—my love?

CANDIDA (with serious vexation). My own particular pet scrubbing brush has been used for blackleading. (A heart-breaking wail bursts from Marchbanks Burgess looks round, amazed. Candida hurries to the sofa.) What's the matter? Are you ill, Eugene?

MARCHBANKS. No, not ill. Only horror, horror, horror! (He bows his head on his hands.)

BURGESS (shocked). What! Got the 'orrors, Mr. Morchbanks! Oh, that's bad, at your age. You must leave it off grajally.

CANDIDA (reassured). Nonsense,

papa. It's only poetic horror, isn't it, Eugene? (Petting him.)

BURGESS (abashed). Oh, poetic 'orror, is it? I beg your pordon, I'm shore. (He turns to the fire again, deprecating his hasty conclusion.)

CANDIDA. What is it, Eugene—the scrubbing brush? (He shudders.) Well, there! never mind. (She sits down beside him.) Wouldn't you like to present me with a nice new one, with an ivory back inlaid with mother-of-pearl?

MARCHBANKS (softly and musically, but sadly and longingly). No, not a scrubbing brush, but a boat—a tiny shallop to sail away in, far from the world, where the marble floors are washed by the rain and dried by the sun, where the south wind dusts the beautiful green and purple carpets. Or a chariot—to carry us up into the sky, where the lamps are stars, and don't need to be filled with paraffin oil every day.

MORELL (harshly). And where there is nothing to do but to be idle, selfish and useless.

CANDIDA (jarred). Oh, James, how could you spoil it all!

MARCHBANKS (firing up). Yes, to be idle, selfish and useless: that is to be beautiful and free and happy: hasn't every man desired that with all his soul for the woman he loves? That's my ideal: what's yours, and that of all the dreadful people who live in these hideous rows of houses? Sermons and scrubbing brushes! With you to preach the sermon and your wife to scrub.

CANDIDA (quaintly). He cleans the boots, Eugene. You will have to clean them to-morrow for saying that about him.

MARCHBANKS. Oh! don't talk about boots. Your feet should be beautiful on the mountains.

CANDIDA. My feet would not be beautiful on the Hackney Road without boots.

BURGESS (scandalized). Come, Candy, don't be vulgar. Mr. Morchbanks ain't accustomed to it. You're givin' him the 'orrors again. I mean the poetic ones.

(Morell is silent. Apparently he is busy with his letters: really he is puzzling with misgiving over his new and alarming experience that the surer he is of his moral thrusts, the more swiftly and effectively Eugene parries them. To find himself beginning to fear a man whom he does not respect affects him bitterly.)

(Miss Garnett comes in with a telegram.)

PROSERPINE (handing the telegram to Morell). Reply paid. The boy's waiting. (To Candida, coming back to her machine and sitting down.) Maria is ready for you now in the kitchen, Mrs. Morell. (Candida rises.) The onions have come.

MARCHBANKS (convulsively). Onions!

CANDIDA. Yes, onions. Not even Spanish ones—nasty little red onions. You shall help me to slice them. Come along.

(She catches him by the wrist and runs out, pulling him after her. Burgess rises in consternation, and stands aghast on the hearth-rug, staring after them.)

BURGESS. Candy didn't oughter 'andle a peer's nevvy like that. It's goin' too fur with it. Lookee 'ere, James: do 'e often git taken queer like that?

MORELL (shortly, writing a telegram). I don't know.

BURGESS (sentimentally). He talks very pretty. I allus had a turn for a bit of potery. Candy takes arter me that-away: huse ter make me tell her fairy stories when she was on'y a little kiddy not that 'igh (indicating a stature of two feet or thereabouts).

MORELL (preoccupied). Ah, indeed. (He blots the telegram, and goes out.)

PROSERPINE. Used you to make the fairy stories up out of your own head?

(Burgess, not deigning to reply, strikes an attitude of the haughtiest disdain on the hearth-rug.)

PROSERPINE (calmly). I should never have supposed you had it in you. By the way, I'd better warn you, since you've taken such a fancy to Mr. Marchbanks. He's mad.

BURGESS. Mad! Wot! 'Im too!!

PROSERPINE. Mad as a March hare. He did frighten me, I can tell you just before you came in that time. Haven't you noticed the queer things he says?

BURGESS. So that's wot the poetic 'orrors means. Blame me if it didn't come into my head once or twyst that he must be off his chump! (He crosses the room to the door, lifting up his voice as he goes.) Well, this is a pretty sort of asylum for a man to be in, with no one but you to take care of him!

PROSERPINE (as he passes her). Yes, what a dreadful thing it would be if anything happened to YOU!

BURGESS (loftily). Don't you address no remarks to me. Tell your hemployer that I've gone into the garden for a smoke.

PROSERPINE (mocking). Oh!

(Before Burgess can retort, Morell comes back.)

BURGESS (sentimentally). Goin' for a turn in the garden to smoke, James.

MORELL (brusquely). Oh, all right, all right. (Burgess goes out pathetically in the character of the weary old man. Morell stands at the table, turning over his papers, and adding, across to Proserpine, half humorously, half absently) Well, Miss Prossy, why have you been calling my father-in-law names?

PROSERPINE (blushing fiery red, and looking quickly up at him, half scared, half reproachful). I— (She bursts into tears.)

MORELL (with tender gaiety, leaning across the table towards her, and consoling her). Oh, come, come, come! Never mind, Pross: he IS a silly old fathead, isn't he?

(With an explosive sob, she makes a dash at the door, and vanishes, banging it. Morell, shaking his head resignedly, sighs, and goes wearily to his chair, where he sits down and sets to work, looking old and careworn.)

(Candida comes in. She has finished her household work and taken of the apron. She at once notices his dejected appearance, and posts herself quietly at the spare chair, looking down at him attentively; but she says nothing.)

MORELL (looking up, but with his pen raised ready to resume his work).

Well? Where is Eugene?

CANDIDA. Washing his hands in the scullery—under the tap. He will make an excellent cook if he can only get over his dread of Maria.

MORELL (shortly). Ha! No doubt. (He begins writing again.)

CANDIDA (going nearer, and putting her hand down softly on his to stop him, as she says). Come here, dear. Let me look at you. (He drops his pen and yields himself at her disposal. She makes him rise and brings him a little away from the table, looking at him critically all the time.) Turn your face to the light. (She places him facing the window.) My boy is not looking well. Has he been overworking?

MORELL. Nothing more than usual.

CANDIDA. He looks very pale, and grey, and wrinkled, and old. (His melancholy deepens; and she attacks it with wilful gaiety.) Here (pulling him towards the easy chair) you've done enough writing for to-day. Leave Prossy to finish it and come and talk to me.

MORELL. But—

CANDIDA. Yes, I MUST be talked to sometimes. (She makes him sit down, and seats herself on the carpet beside his knee.) Now (patting his hand) you're beginning to look better already. Why don't you give up all this tiresome overworking—going out every night lecturing and talking? Of course what you say is all very true and very right; but it does no good: they don't mind what you say to them one little bit. Of course they agree with you; but what's the use of people agreeing with you if they go and do just the opposite of what you tell them the moment your back is turned? Look at our congregation at St. Dominic's! Why do they come to hear you talking about Christianity every Sunday? Why, just because they've been so full of business and money-making for six days that they want to forget all about it and have a rest on the seventh, so that they can go back fresh and make money harder than ever! You positively help them at it instead of hindering them.

MORELL (with energetic seriousness). You know very well, Candida, that I often blow them up soundly for that. But if there is nothing in their church-going but rest and diversion, why don't they try something more amusing—more self-indulgent? There must be some good in the fact that they prefer St. Dominic's to worse places on Sundays.

CANDIDA. Oh, the worst places aren't open; and even if they were, they daren't be seen going to them. Besides, James, dear, you preach so splendidly that it's as good as a play for them. Why do you think the women are so enthusiastic?

MORELL (shocked). Candida!

CANDIDA. Oh, *I* know. You silly boy: you think it's your Socialism and your religion; but if it was that, they'd do what you tell them instead of only coming to look at you. They all have Prossy's complaint.

MORELL. Prossy's complaint! What do you mean, Candida?

CANDIDA. Yes, Prossy, and all the other secretaries you ever had. Why does Prossy condescend to wash up the things, and to peel potatoes and abase herself in all manner of ways for six shillings a week less than she used to get in a city office? She's in love with you, James: that's the reason. They're all in love with you. And you are in love with preaching because you do it so beautifully. And you think it's all enthusiasm for the kingdom of Heaven on earth; and so do they. You dear silly!

MORELL. Candida: what dreadful, what soul-destroying cynicism! Are you jesting? Or—can it be?—are you jealous?

CANDIDA (with curious thoughtfulness). Yes, I feel a little jealous sometimes.

MORELL (incredulously). What! Of Prossy?

CANDIDA (laughing). No, no, no, no. Not jealous of anybody. Jealous for somebody else, who is not loved as he ought to be.

MORELL. Me!

CANDIDA. You! Why, you're spoiled with love and worship: you get far more than is good for you. No: I mean Eugene.

MORELL (startled). Eugene!

CANDIDA. It seems unfair that all the love should go to you, and none to him, although he needs it so much more than you do. (A convulsive movement shakes him in spite of himself.) What's the matter? Am I worrying you?

MORELL (hastily). Not at all. (Looking at her with troubled intensity.) You know that I have perfect confidence in you, Candida.

CANDIDA. You vain thing! Are you so sure of your irresistible attractions?

MORELL. Candida: you are shocking me. I never thought of my attractions I thought of your goodness—your purity. That is what I confide in.

CANDIDA. What a nasty, uncomfortable thing to say to me! Oh, you ARE a clergyman, James—a thorough clergyman.

MORELL (turning away from her, heart-stricken). So Eugene says.

CANDIDA (with lively interest, leaning over to him with her arms on his knee). Eugene's always right. He's a wonderful boy: I have grown fonder and fonder of him all the time I was away. Do you know, James, that though he has not the least suspicion of it himself, he is ready to fall madly in love with me?

MORELL (grimly). Oh, he has no suspicion of it himself, hasn't he?

CANDIDA. Not a bit (She takes her arms from his knee, and turns thoughtfully, sinking into a more restful attitude with her hands in her lap.) Some day he will know when he is grown up and experienced, like you. And he will know that I must have known. I wonder what he will think of me then.

MORELL. No evil, Candida. I hope and trust, no evil.

CANDIDA (dubiously). That will depend.

MORELL (bewildered). Depend!

CANDIDA (looking at him). Yes: it will depend on what happens to him. (He look vacantly at her.) Don't you see? It will depend on how he comes to learn what love really is. I mean on the sort of woman who will teach it to him.

MORELL (quite at a loss). Yes. No. I don't know what you mean.

CANDIDA (explaining). If he learns

it from a good woman, then it will be all right: he will forgive me.

MORELL. Forgive!

CANDIDA. But suppose he learns it from a bad woman, as so many men do, especially poetic men, who imagine all women are angels! Suppose he only discovers the value of love when he has thrown it away and degraded himself in his ignorance. Will he forgive me then, do you think?

MORELL. Forgive you for what?

CANDIDA (realizing how stupid he is, and a little disappointed, though quite tenderly so). Don't you understand? (He shakes his head. She turns to him again, so as to explain with the fondest intimacy.) I mean, will he forgive me for not teaching him myself? For abandoning him to the bad women for the sake of my goodness—my purity, as you call it? Ah, James, how little you understand me, to talk of your confidence in my goodness and purity! I would give them both to poor Eugene as willingly as I would give my shawl to a beggar dying of cold, if there were nothing else to restrain me. Put your trust in my love for you, James, for if that went, I should care very little for your sermons—mere phrases that you cheat yourself and others with every day. (She is about to rise.)

MORELL. HIS words!

CANDIDA (checking herself quickly in the act of getting up, so that she is on her knees, but upright). Whose words?

MORELL. Eugene's.

CANDIDA (delighted). He is always right. He understands you; he understands me; he understands Prossy; and you, James—you understand nothing. (She laughs, and kisses him to console him. He recoils as if stung, and springs up.)

MORELL. How can you bear to do that when—oh, Candida (with anguish in his voice) I had rather you had plunged a grappling iron into my heart than given me that kiss.

CANDIDA (rising, alarmed). My dear: what's the matter?

MORELL (frantically waving her off). Don't touch me.

CANDIDA (amazed). James!

(They are interrupted by the entrance of Marchbanks, with Burgess, who stops near the door, staring, whilst Eugene hurries forward between them.)

MARCHBANKS. Is anything the matter?

MORELL (deadly white, putting an iron constraint on himself). Nothing but this: that either you were right this morning, or Candida is mad.

BURGESS (in loudest protest). Wot! Candy mad too! Oh, come, come, come! (He crosses the room to the fireplace, protesting as he goes, and knocks the ashes out of his pipe on the bars. Morell sits down desperately, leaning forward to hide his face, and interlacing his fingers rigidly to keep them steady.)

CANDIDA (to Morell, relieved and laughing). Oh, you're only shocked! Is that all? How conventional all you unconventional people are!

BURGESS. Come: be'ave yourself, Candy. What'll Mr. Morchbanks think of you?

CANDIDA. This comes of James teaching me to think for myself, and never to hold back out of fear of what other people may think of me. It works beautifully as long as I think the same things as he does. But now, because I have just thought something different!—look at him—just look!

(She points to Morell, greatly amused. Eugene looks, and instantly presses his band on his heart, as if some deadly pain had shot through it, and sits down on the sofa like a man witnessing a tragedy.)

BURGESS (on the hearth-rug). Well, James, you certainly ain't as himpressive lookin' as usu'l.

MORELL (with a laugh which is half a sob). I suppose not. I beg all your pardons: I was not conscious of making a fuss. (Pulling himself together.) Well, well, well, well, well! (He goes back to his place at the table, setting to work at his papers again with resolute cheerfulness.)

CANDIDA (going to the sofa and sitting beside Marchbanks, still in a bantering humor). Well, Eugene, why are you so sad? Did the onions make you cry?

(Morell cannot prevent himself from watching them.)

MARCHBANKS (aside to her). It is your cruelty. I hate cruelty. It is a horrible thing to see one person make another suffer.

CANDIDA (petting him ironically). Poor boy, have I been cruel? Did I make it slice nasty little red onions?

MARCHBANKS (earnestly). Oh, stop, stop: I don't mean myself. You have made him suffer frightfully. I feel his pain in my own heart. I know that it is not your fault—it is something that must happen; but don't make light of it. I shudder when you torture him and laugh.

CANDIDA (incredulously). I torture James! Nonsense, Eugene: how you exaggerate! Silly! (She looks round at Morell, who hastily resumes his writing. She goes to him and stands behind his chair, bending over him.) Don't work any more, dear. Come and talk to us.

MORELL (affectionately but bitterly). Ah no: I can't talk. I can only preach.

CANDIDA (caressing him). Well, come and preach.

BURGESS (strongly remonstrating). Aw, no, Candy. 'Ang it all! (Lexy Mill comes in, looking anxious and important.)

LEXY (hastening to shake hands with Candida). How do you do, Mrs. Morell? So glad to see you back again.

CANDIDA. Thank you, Lexy. You know Eugene, don't you?

LEXY. Oh, yes. How do you do, Marchbanks?

MARCHBANKS. Quite well, thanks.

LEXY (to Morell). I've just come from the Guild of St. Matthew. They are in the greatest consternation about your telegram. There's nothing wrong, is there?

CANDIDA. What did you telegraph about, James?

LEXY (to Candida). He was to have spoken for them tonight. They've taken the large hall in Mare Street and spent a lot of money on posters. Morell's telegram was to say he couldn't come.

It came on them like a thunderbolt.

CANDIDA (surprised, and beginning to suspect something wrong). Given up an engagement to speak!

BURGESS. First time in his life, I'll bet. Ain' it, Candy?

LEXY (to Morell). They decided to send an urgent telegram to you asking whether you could not change your mind. Have you received it?

MORELL (with restrained impatience). Yes, yes: I got it.

LEXY. It was reply paid.

MORELL. Yes, I know. I answered it. I can't go.

CANDIDA. But why, James?

MORELL (almost fiercely). Because I don't choose. These people forget that I am a man: they think I am a talking machine to be turned on for their pleasure every evening of my life. May I not have ONE night at home, with my wife, and my friends?

(They are all amazed at this outburst, except Eugene. His expression remains unchanged.)

CANDIDA. Oh, James, you know you'll have an attack of bad conscience to-morrow; and *I* shall have to suffer for that.

LEXY (intimidated, but urgent). I know, of course, that they make the most unreasonable demands on you. But they have been telegraphing all over the place for another speaker: and they can get nobody but the President of the Agnostic League.

MORELL (promptly). Well, an excellent man. What better do they want?

LEXY. But he always insists so powerfully on the divorce of Socialism from Christianity. He will undo all the good we have been doing. Of course you know best; but—(He hesitates.)

CANDIDA (coaxingly). Oh, DO go, James. We'll all go.

BURGESS (grumbling). Look 'ere, Candy! I say! Let's stay at home by the fire, comfortable. He won't need to be more'n a couple-o'-hour away.

CANDIDA. You'll be just as comfortable at the meeting. We'll all sit on the platform and be great people.

EUGENE (terrified). Oh, please don't let us go on the platform. No—everyone will stare at us—I couldn't. I'll sit at the back of the room.

CANDIDA. Don't be afraid. They'll be too busy looking at James to notice you.

MORELL (turning his head and looking meaningly at her over his shoulder). Prossy's complaint, Candida! Eh?

CANDIDA (gaily). Yes.

BURGESS (mystified). Prossy's complaint. Wot are you talking about, James?

MORELL (not heeding him, rises; goes to the door; and holds it open, shouting in a commanding voice). Miss Garnett.

PROSERPINE (in the distance). Yes, Mr. Morell. Coming. (They all wait, except Burgess, who goes stealthily to Lexy and draws him aside.)

BURGESS. Listen here, Mr. Mill. Wot's Prossy's complaint? Wot's wrong with 'er?

LEXY (confidentially). Well, I don't exactly know; but she spoke very strangely to me this morning. I'm afraid she's a little out of her mind sometimes.

BURGESS (overwhelmed). Why, it must be catchin'! Four in the same 'ouse! (He goes back to the hearth, quite lost before the instability of the human intellect in a clergyman's house.)

PROSERPINE (appearing on the threshold). What is it, Mr. Morell?

MORELL. Telegraph to the Guild of St. Matthew that I am coming.

PROSERPINE (surprised). Don't they expect you?

MORELL (peremptorily). Do as I tell you.

(Proserpine frightened, sits down at her typewriter, and obeys. Morell goes across to Burgess, Candida watching his movements all the time with growing wonder and misgiving.)

MORELL. Burgess: you don't want to come?

BURGESS (in deprecation). Oh, don't put it like that, James. It's only that it ain't Sunday, you know.

MORELL. I'm sorry. I thought you might like to be introduced to the chairman. He's on the Works Committee of the County Council and has some influence in the matter of contracts. (Burgess wakes up at once. Morell, expecting as much, waits a moment, and says) Will you come?

BURGESS (with enthusiasm). Course I'll come, James. Ain' it always a pleasure to 'ear you.

MORELL (turning from him). I shall want you to take some notes at the meeting, Miss Garnett, if you have no other engagement. (She nods, afraid to speak.) You are coming, Lexy, I suppose.

LEXY. Certainly.

CANDIDA. We are all coming, James.

MORELL. No: you are not coming; and Eugene is not coming. You will stay here and entertain him—to celebrate your return home. (Eugene rises, breathless.)

CANDIDA. But James—

MORELL (authoritatively). I insist. You do not want to come; and he does not want to come. (Candida is about to protest.) Oh, don't concern yourselves: I shall have plenty of people without you: your chairs will be wanted by unconverted people who have never heard me before.

CANDIDA (troubled). Eugene: wouldn't you like to come?

MORELL. I should be afraid to let myself go before Eugene: he is so critical of sermons. (Looking at him.) He knows I am afraid of him: he told me as much this morning. Well, I shall show him how much afraid I am by leaving him here in your custody, Candida.

MARCHBANKS (to himself, with vivid feeling). That's brave. That's beautiful. (He sits down again listening with parted lips.)

CANDIDA (with anxious misgiving). But—but—Is anything the matter, James? (Greatly troubled.) I can't understand—

MORELL. Ah, I thought it was I who couldn't understand, dear. (He takes her tenderly in his arms and kisses her on the forehead; then looks round quietly at Marchbanks.)

ACT III

Late in the evening. Past ten. The curtains are drawn, and the lamps lighted. The typewriter is in its case; the large table has been cleared and tidied; everything indicates that the day's work is done.

Candida and Marchbanks are seated at the fire. The reading lamp is on the mantelshelf above Marchbanks, who is sitting on the small chair reading aloud from a manuscript. A little pile of manuscripts and a couple of volumes of poetry are on the carpet beside him. Candida is in the easy chair with the poker, a light brass one, upright in her hand. She is leaning back and looking at the point of it curiously, with her feet stretched towards the blaze and her heels resting on the fender, profoundly unconscious of her appearance and surroundings.

MARCHBANKS (breaking off in his recitation): Every poet that ever lived has put that thought into a sonnet. He must: he can't help it. (He looks to her for assent, and notices her absorption in the poker.) Haven't you been listening? (No response.) Mrs. Morell!

CANDIDA (starting). Eh?

MARCHBANKS. Haven't you been listening?

CANDIDA (with a guilty excess of politeness). Oh, yes. It's very nice. Go on, Eugene. I'm longing to hear what happens to the angel.

MARCHBANKS (crushed—the manuscript dropping from his hand to the floor). I beg your pardon for boring you.

CANDIDA. But you are not boring me, I assure you. Please go on. Do, Eugene.

MARCHBANKS. I finished the poem about the angel quarter of an hour ago. I've read you several things since.

CANDIDA (remorsefully). I'm so sorry, Eugene. I think the poker must have fascinated me. (She puts it down.)

MARCHBANKS. It made me horribly uneasy.

CANDIDA. Why didn't you tell me? I'd have put it down at once.

MARCHBANKS. I was afraid of making you uneasy, too. It looked as if it were a weapon. If I were a hero of old, I should have laid my drawn sword between us. If Morell had come in he would have thought you had taken up the poker because there was no sword between us.

CANDIDA (wondering). What? (With a puzzled glance at him.) I can't quite follow that. Those sonnets of yours have perfectly addled me. Why should there be a sword between us?

MARCHBANKS (evasively). Oh, never mind. (He stoops to pick up the manuscript.)

CANDIDA. Put that down again, Eugene. There are limits to my appetite for poetry—even your poetry. You've been reading to me for more than two hours—ever since James went out. I want to talk.

MARCHBANKS (rising, scared). No: I mustn't talk. (He looks round him in his lost way, and adds, suddenly) I think I'll go out and take a walk in the park. (Making for the door.)

CANDIDA. Nonsense: it's shut long ago. Come and sit down on the hearth-rug, and talk moonshine as you usually do. I want to be amused. Don't you want to?

MARCHBANKS (in half terror, half rapture). Yes.

CANDIDA. Then come along. (She moves her chair back a little to make room. He hesitates; then timidly stretches himself on the hearth-rug, face upwards, and throws back his head across her knees, looking up at her.)

MARCHBANKS. Oh, I've been so miserable all the evening, because I was doing right. Now I'm doing wrong; and I'm happy.

CANDIDA (tenderly amused at him). Yes: I'm sure you feel a great grown up wicked deceiver—quite proud of yourself, aren't you?

MARCHBANKS (raising his head quickly and turning a little to look round at her). Take care. I'm ever so much older than you, if you only knew. (He turns quite over on his knees, with his hands clasped and his arms on her lap, and speaks with growing impulse, his blood beginning to stir.) May I say some wicked things to you?

CANDIDA (without the least fear or coldness, quite nobly, and with perfect respect for his passion, but with a touch of her wise-hearted maternal humor). No. But you may say anything you really and truly feel. Anything at all, no matter what it is. I am not afraid, so long as it is your real self that speaks, and not a mere attitude—a gallant attitude, or a wicked attitude, or even a poetic attitude. I put you on your honor and truth. Now say whatever you want to.

MARCHBANKS (the eager expression vanishing utterly from his lips and nostrils as his eyes light up with pathetic spirituality). Oh, now I can't say anything: all the words I know belong to some attitude or other—all except one.

CANDIDA. What one is that?

MARCHBANKS (softly, losing himself in the music of the name). Candida, Candida, Candida, Candida, Candida. I must say that now, because you have put me on my honor and truth; and I never think or feel Mrs. Morell: it is always Candida.

CANDIDA. Of course. And what have you to say to Candida?

MARCHBANKS. Nothing, but to repeat your name a thousand times. Don't you feel that every time is a prayer to you?

CANDIDA. Doesn't it make you happy to be able to pray?

MARCHBANKS. Yes, very happy.

CANDIDA. Well, that happiness is the answer to your prayer. Do you want anything more?

MARCHBANKS (in beatitude). No: I have come into heaven, where want is unknown.

(Morell comes in. He halts on the threshold, and takes in the scene at a glance.)

MORELL (grave and self-contained). I hope I don't disturb you. (Candida starts up violently, but without the smallest embarrassment, laughing at herself. Eugene, still kneeling, saves himself from falling by putting his hands on the seat of the chair, and remains there, staring open mouthed at Morell.)

CANDIDA (as she rises). Oh, James, how you startled me! I was so taken up with Eugene that I didn't hear your latch-key. How did the meeting go off?

Did you speak well?

MORELL. I have never spoken better in my life.

CANDIDA. That was first rate! How much was the collection?

MORELL. I forgot to ask.

CANDIDA (to Eugene). He must have spoken splendidly, or he would never have forgotten that. (To Morell.) Where are all the others?

MORELL. They left long before I could get away: I thought I should never escape. I believe they are having supper somewhere.

CANDIDA (in her domestic business tone). Oh; in that case, Maria may go to bed. I'll tell her. (She goes out to the kitchen.)

MORELL (looking sternly down at Marchbanks). Well?

MARCHBANKS (squatting cross-legged on the hearth-rug, and actually at ease with Morell—even impishly humorous). Well?

MORELL. Have you anything to tell me?

MARCHBANKS. Only that I have been making a fool of myself here in private whilst you have been making a fool of yourself in public.

MORELL. Hardly in the same way, I think.

MARCHBANKS (scrambling up—eagerly). The very, very, VERY same way. I have been playing the good man just like you. When you began your heroics about leaving me here with Candida—

MORELL (involuntarily). Candida?

MARCHBANKS. Oh, yes: I've got that far. Heroics are infectious: I caught the disease from you. I swore not to say a word in your absence that I would not have said a month ago in your presence.

MORELL. Did you keep your oath?

MARCHBANKS. (suddenly perching himself grotesquely on the easy chair). I was ass enough to keep it until about ten minutes ago. Up to that moment I went on desperately reading to her—reading my own poems—anybody's poems—to stave off a conversation. I was standing outside the gate of Heaven, and refusing to go in. Oh, you can't think how heroic it was, and how uncomfortable! Then—

MORELL (steadily controlling his suspense). Then?

MARCHBANKS (prosaically slipping down into a quite ordinary attitude in the chair). Then she couldn't bear being read to any longer.

MORELL. And you approached the gate of Heaven at last?

MARCHBANKS. Yes.

MORELL. Well? (Fiercely.) Speak, man: have you no feeling for me?

MARCHBANKS (softly and musically). Then she became an angel; and there was a flaming sword that turned every way, so that I couldn't go in; for I saw that that gate was really the gate of Hell.

MORELL (triumphantly). She repulsed you!

MARCHBANKS (rising in wild scorn). No, you fool: if she had done that I should never have seen that I was in Heaven already. Repulsed me! You think that would have saved me—virtuous indignation! Oh, you are not worthy to live in the same world with her. (He turns away contemptuously to the other side of the room.)

MORELL (who has watched him quietly without changing his place). Do you think you make yourself more worthy by reviling me, Eugene?

MARCHBANKS. Here endeth the thousand and first lesson. Morell: I don't think much of your preaching after all: I believe I could do it better myself. The man I want to meet is the man that Candida married.

MORELL. The man that—? Do you mean me?

MARCHBANKS. I don't mean the Reverend James Mavor Morell, moralist and windbag. I mean the real man that the Reverend James must have hidden somewhere inside his black coat—the man that Candida loved. You can't make a woman like Candida love you by merely buttoning your collar at the back instead of in front.

MORELL (boldly and steadily). When Candida promised to marry me, I was the same moralist and windbag that you now see. I wore my black coat; and my collar was buttoned behind instead of in front. Do you think she would have loved me any the better for being insincere in my profession?

MARCHBANKS (on the sofa hugging his ankles). Oh, she forgave you, just as she forgives me for being a coward, and a weakling, and what you call a snivelling little whelp and all the rest of it. (Dreamily.) A woman like that has divine insight: she loves our souls, and not our follies and vanities and illusions, or our collars and coats, or any other of the rags and tatters we are rolled up in. (He reflects on this for an instant; then turns intently to question Morell.) What I want to know is how you got past the flaming sword that stopped me.

MORELL (meaningly). Perhaps because I was not interrupted at the end of ten minutes.

MARCHBANKS (taken aback). What!

MORELL. Man can climb to the highest summits; but he cannot dwell there long.

MARCHBANKS. It's false: there can he dwell for ever and there only. It's in the other moments that he can find no rest, no sense of the silent glory of life. Where would you have me spend my moments, if not on the summits?

MORELL. In the scullery, slicing onions and filling lamps.

MARCHBANKS. Or in the pulpit, scrubbing cheap earthenware souls?

MORELL. Yes, that, too. It was there that I earned my golden moment, and the right, in that moment, to ask her to love me. I did not take the moment on credit; nor did I use it to steal another man's happiness.

MARCHBANKS (rather disgustedly, trotting back towards the fireplace). I have no doubt you conducted the transaction as honestly as if you were buying a pound of cheese. (He stops on the brink of the hearth-rug and adds, thoughtfully, to himself, with his back turned to Morell) I could only go to her as a beggar.

MORELL (starting). A beggar dying of cold—asking for her shawl?

MARCHBANKS (turning, surprised). Thank you for touching up my poetry. Yes, if you like, a beggar dying of cold asking for her shawl.

MORELL (excitedly). And she refused. Shall I tell you why she refused? I CAN tell you, on her own authority. It was because of—

MARCHBANKS. She didn't refuse.

MORELL. Not!

MARCHBANKS. She offered me all I chose to ask for, her shawl, her wings, the wreath of stars on her head, the lilies in her hand, the crescent moon beneath her feet—

MORELL (seizing him). Out with the truth, man: my wife is my wife: I want no more of your poetic fripperies. I know well that if I have lost her love and you have gained it, no law will bind her.

MARCHBANKS (quaintly, without fear or resistance). Catch me by the shirt collar, Morell: she will arrange it for me afterwards as she did this morning. (With quiet rapture.) I shall feel her hands touch me.

MORELL. You young imp, do you know how dangerous it is to say that to me? Or (with a sudden misgiving) has something made you brave?

MARCHBANKS. I'm not afraid now. I disliked you before: that was why I shrank from your touch. But I saw to-day—when she tortured you—that you love her. Since then I have been your friend: you may strangle me if you like.

MORELL (releasing him). Eugene: if that is not a heartless lie—if you have a spark of human feeling left in you—will you tell me what has happened during my absence?

MARCHBANKS. What happened! Why, the flaming sword—(Morell stamps with impatience.) Well, in plain prose, I loved her so exquisitely that I wanted nothing more than the happiness of being in such love. And before I had time to come down from the highest summits, you came in.

MORELL (suffering deeply). So it is still unsettled—still the misery of doubt.

MARCHBANKS. Misery! I am the happiest of men. I desire nothing now but her happiness. (With dreamy enthusiasm.) Oh, Morell, let us both give her up. Why should she have to choose between a wretched little nervous disease like me, and a pig-headed parson like you? Let us go on a pilgrimage, you to the east and I to the west, in search of a worthy lover for her—some beautiful archangel with purple wings—

MORELL. Some fiddlestick. Oh, if she is mad enough to leave me for you, who will protect her? Who will help her? who will work for her? who will be a father to her children? (He sits down distractedly on the sofa, with his elbows on his knees and his head propped on his clenched fists.)

MARCHBANKS (snapping his fingers wildly). She does not ask those silly questions. It is she who wants somebody to protect, to help, to work for—somebody to give her children to protect, to help and to work for. Some grown up man who has become as a little child again. Oh, you fool, you fool, you triple fool! I am the man, Morell: I am the man. (He dances about excitedly, crying.) You don't understand what a woman is. Send for her, Morell: send for her and let her choose between—(The door opens and Candida enters. He stops as if petrified.)

CANDIDA (amazed, on the threshold). What on earth are you at, Eugene?

MARCHBANKS (oddly). James and I are having a preaching match; and he is getting the worst of it. (Candida looks quickly round at Morell. Seeing that he is distressed, she hurries down to him, greatly vexed, speaking with vigorous reproach to Marchbanks.)

CANDIDA. You have been annoying him. Now I won't have it, Eugene: do you hear? (Putting her hand on Morell's shoulder, and quite forgetting her wifely tact in her annoyance.) My boy shall not be worried: I will protect him.

MORELL (rising proudly). Protect!

CANDIDA (not heeding him—to Eugene). What have you been saying?

MARCHBANKS (appalled). Nothing—

CANDIDA. Eugene! Nothing?

MARCHBANKS (piteously). I mean—I—I'm very sorry. I won't do it again: indeed I won't. I'll let him alone.

MORELL (indignantly, with an aggressive movement towards Eugene). Let me alone! You young—

CANDIDA (Stopping him). Sh—no, let me deal with him, James.

MARCHBANKS. Oh, you're not angry with me, are you?

CANDIDA (severely). Yes, I am—very angry. I have a great mind to pack you out of the house.

MORELL (taken aback by Candida's vigor, and by no means relishing the sense of being rescued by her from another man). Gently, Candida, gently. I am able to take care of myself.

CANDIDA (petting him). Yes, dear: of course you are. But you mustn't be annoyed and made miserable.

MARCHBANKS (almost in tears, turning to the door). I'll go.

CANDIDA. Oh, you needn't go: I can't turn you out at this time of night. (Vehemently.) Shame on you! For shame!

MARCHBANKS (desperately). But what have I done?

CANDIDA. I know what you have done—as well as if I had been here all the time. Oh, it was unworthy! You are like a child: you cannot hold your tongue.

MARCHBANKS. I would die ten times over sooner than give you a moment's pain.

CANDIDA (with infinite contempt for this puerility). Much good your dying would do me!

MORELL. Candida, my dear: this altercation is hardly quite seemingly. It is a matter between two men; and I am the right person to settle it.

CANDIDA. Two MEN! Do you call that a man? (To Eugene.) You bad boy!

MARCHBANKS (gathering a whimsically affectionate courage from the scolding). If I am to be scolded like this, I must make a boy's excuse. He began it. And he's bigger than I am.

CANDIDA (losing confidence a little as her concern for Morell's dignity takes the alarm). That can't be true. (To Morell.) You didn't begin it, James, did you?

MORELL (contemptuously). No.

MARCHBANKS (indignant). Oh!

MORELL (to Eugene). YOU began

it—this morning. (Candida, instantly connecting this with his mysterious allusion in the afternoon to something told him by Eugene in the morning, looks quickly at him, wrestling with the enigma. Morell proceeds with the emphasis of offended superiority.) But your other point is true. I am certainly the bigger of the two, and, I hope, the stronger, Candida. So you had better leave the matter in my hands.

CANDIDA (again soothing him). Yes, dear; but—(Troubled.) I don't understand about this morning.

MORELL (gently snubbing her). You need not understand, my dear.

CANDIDA. But, James, I—(The street bell rings.) Oh, bother! Here they all come. (She goes out to let them in.)

MARCHBANKS (running to Morell). Oh, Morell, isn't it dreadful? She's angry with us: she hates me. What shall I do?

MORELL (with quaint desperation, clutching himself by the hair). Eugene: my head is spinning round. I shall begin to laugh presently. (He walks up and down the middle of the room.)

MARCHBANKS (following him anxiously). No, no: she'll think I've thrown you into hysterics. Don't laugh. (Boisterous voices and laughter are heard approaching. Lexy Mill, his eyes sparkling, and his bearing denoting unwonted elevation of spirit, enters with Burgess, who is greasy and self-complacent, but has all his wits about him. Miss Garnett, with her smartest hat and jacket on, follows them; but though her eyes are brighter than before, she is evidently a prey to misgiving. She places herself with her back to her typewriting table, with one hand on it to rest herself, passes the other across her forehead as if she were a little tired and giddy. Marchbanks relapses into shyness and edges away into the corner near the window, where Morell's books are.)

MILL (exhilaratedly). Morell: I MUST congratulate you. (Grasping his hand.) What a noble, splendid, inspired address you gave us! You surpassed yourself.

BURGESS. So you did, James. It fair kep' me awake to the last word. Didn't it, Miss Garnett?

PROSERPINE (worriedly). Oh, I wasn't minding you: I was trying to make notes. (She takes out her notbook, and looks at her stenography, which nearly makes her cry.)

MORELL. Did I go too fast, Pross?

PROSERPINE. Much too fast. You know I can't do more than a hundred words a minute. (She relieves her feelings by throwing her notbook angrily beside her machine, ready for use next morning.)

MORELL (soothingly). Oh, well, well, never mind, never mind, never mind. Have you all had supper?

LEXY. Mr. Burgess has been kind enough to give us a really splendid supper at the Belgrave.

BURGESS (with effusive magnanimity). Don't mention it, Mr. Mill. (Modestly.) You're 'arty welcome to my little treat.

PROSERPINE. We had champagne! I never tasted it before. I feel quite giddy.

MORELL (surprised). A champagne supper! That was very handsome. Was it my eloquence that produced all this extravagance?

MILL (rhetorically). Your eloquence, and Mr. Burgess's goodness of heart. (With a fresh burst of exhilaration.) And what a very fine fellow the chairman is, Morell! He came to supper with us.

MORELL (with long drawn significance, looking at Burgess). O-o-o-h, the chairman. NOW I understand.

(Burgess, covering a lively satisfaction in his diplomatic cunning with a deprecatory cough, retires to the hearth. Lexy folds his arms and leans against the cellaret in a high-spirited attitude. Candida comes in with glasses, lemons, and a jug of hot water on a tray.)

CANDIDA. Who will have some lemonade? You know our rules: total abstinence. (She puts the tray on the table, and takes up the lemon squeezers, looking enquiringly round at them.)

MORELL. No use, dear. They've all had champagne. Pross has broken her pledge.

CANDIDA (to Proserpine). You don't mean to say you've been drinking champagne!

PROSERPINE (stubbornly). Yes, I do. I'm only a beer teetotaller, not a champagne teetotaller. I don't like beer. Are there any letters for me to answer, Mr. Morell?

MORELL. No more to-night.

PROSERPINE. Very well. Goodnight, everybody.

LEXY (gallantly). Had I not better see you home, Miss Garnett?

PROSERPINE. No, thank you. I shan't trust myself with anybody tonight I wish I hadn't taken any of that stuff. (She walks straight out.)

BURGESS (indignantly). Stuff, indeed! That gurl dunno wot champagne is! Pommery and Greeno at twelve and six a bottle. She took two glasses a most straight hoff.

MORELL (a little anxious about her). Go and look after her, Lexy.

LEXY (alarmed). But if she should really be—Suppose she began to sing in the street, or anything of that sort.

MORELL. Just so: she may That's why you'd better see her safely home.

CANDIDA. Do, Lexy: there's a good fellow. (She shakes his hand and pushes him gently to the door.)

LEXY. It's evidently my duty to go. I hope it may not be necessary Goodnight, Mrs. Morell. (To the rest.) Goodnight. (He goes. Candida shuts the door.)

BURGESS. He was gushin' with hextra piety hisself arter two sips. People carn't drink like they huseter. (Dismissing the subject and bustling away from the hearth.) Well, James: it's time to lock up. Mr. Morchbanks: shall I 'ave the pleasure of your company for a bit of the way home?

MARCHBANKS (affrightedly). Yes: I'd better go. (He hurries across to the door; but Candida places herself before it, barring his way.)

CANDIDA (with quiet authority). You sit down. You're not going yet.

MARCHBANKS (quailing). No I— I didn't mean to. (He comes back into the room and sits down abjectly on the sofa.)

CANDIDA. Mr. Marchbanks will stay the night with us, papa.

BURGESS. Oh, well, I'll say goodnight. So long, James. (He shakes hands with Morell and goes on to Eugene.) Make 'em give you a night light by your bed, Mr. Morchbanks: it'll comfort you if you wake up in the night with a touch of that complaint of yores. Good-night.

MARCHBANKS. Thank you: I will. Good-night, Mr. Burgess. (They shake hands and Burgess goes to the door.)

CANDIDA (intercepting Morell, who is following Burgess). Stay here, dear: I'll put on papa's coat for him. (She goes out with Burgess.)

MARCHBANKS. Morell: there's going to be a terrible scene. Aren't you afraid?

MORELL. Not in the least.

MARCHBANKS. I never envied you your courage before. (He rises timidly and puts his hand appealingly on Morell's forearm.) Stand by me, won't you?

MORELL (casting him off gently, but resolutely). Each for himself, Eugene. She must choose between us now. (He goes to the other side of the room as Candida returns. Eugene sits down again on the sofa like a guilty schoolboy on his best behaviour.)

CANDIDA (between them, addressing Eugene). Are you sorry?

MARCHBANKS (earnestly). Yes, heartbroken.

CANDIDA. Well, then, you are forgiven. Now go off to bed like a good little boy: I want to talk to James about you.

MARCHBANKS (rising in great consternation). Oh, I can't do that, Morell. I must be here. I'll not go away. Tell her.

CANDIDA (with quick suspicion). Tell me what? (His eyes avoid hers furtively. She turns and mutely transfers the question to Morell.)

MORELL (bracing himself for the catastrophe). I have nothing to tell her, except (here his voice deepens to a measured and mournful tenderness) that she is my greatest treasure on earth—if she is really mine.

CANDIDA (coldly, offended by his yielding to his orator's instinct and treating her as if she were the audience at the Guild of St. Matthew). I am sure Eugene can say no less, if that is all.

MARCHBANKS (discouraged). Morell: she's laughing at us.

MORELL (with a quick touch of temper). There is nothing to laugh at. Are you laughing at us, Candida?

CANDIDA (with quiet anger). Eugene is very quick-witted, James. I hope I am going to laugh; but I am not sure that I am not going to be very angry. (She goes to the fireplace, and stands there leaning with her arm on the mantelpiece and her foot on the fender, whilst Eugene steals to Morell and plucks him by the sleeve.)

MARCHBANKS (whispering). Stop Morell. Don't let us say anything.

MORELL (pushing Eugene away without deigning to look at him). I hope you don't mean that as a threat, Candida.

CANDIDA (with emphatic warning). Take care, James. Eugene: I asked you to go. Are you going?

MORELL (putting his foot down). He shall not go. I wish him to remain.

MARCHBANKS. I'll go. I'll do whatever you want. (He turns to the door.)

CANDIDA. Stop! (He obeys.) Didn't you hear James say he wished you to stay? James is master here. Don't you know that?

MARCHBANKS (flushing with a young poet's rage against tyranny). By what right is he master?

CANDIDA (quietly). Tell him, James.

MORELL (taken aback). My dear: I don't know of any right that makes me master. I assert no such right.

CANDIDA (with infinite reproach). You don't know! Oh, James, James! (To Eugene, musingly.) I wonder do you understand, Eugene! No: you're too young. Well, I give you leave to stay—to stay and learn. (She comes away from the hearth and places herself between them.) Now, James: what's the matter? Come: tell me.

MARCHBANKS (whispering tremulously across to him). Don't.

CANDIDA. Come. Out with it!

MORELL (slowly). I meant to prepare your mind carefully, Candida, so as to prevent misunderstanding.

CANDIDA. Yes, dear: I am sure you did. But never mind: I shan't misunderstand.

MORELL. Well—er—(He hesitates, unable to find the long explanation which he supposed to be available.)

CANDIDA. Well?

MORELL (baldly). Eugene declares that you are in love with him.

MARCHBANKS (frantically). No, no, no, no, never. I did not, Mrs. Morell: it's not true. I said I loved you, and that he didn't. I said that I understood you, and that he couldn't. And it was not after what passed there before the fire that I spoke: it was not, on my word. It was this morning.

CANDIDA (enlightened). This morning!

MARCHBANKS. Yes. (He looks at her, pleading for credence, and then adds, simply) That was what was the matter with my collar.

CANDIDA (after a pause; for she does not take in his meaning at once). His collar! (She turns to Morell, shocked.) Oh, James: did you—(she stops)?

MORELL (ashamed). You know, Candida, that I have a temper to struggle with. And he said (shuddering) that you despised me in your heart.

CANDIDA (turning quickly on Eugene). Did you say that?

MARCHBANKS (terrified). No!

CANDIDA (severely). Then James has just told me a falsehood. Is that what you mean?

MARCHBANKS. No, no: I—I—(blurting out the explanation desperately) —it was David's wife. And it wasn't at home: it was when she saw him dancing before all the people.

MORELL (taking the cue with a debater's adroitness). Dancing before all the people, Candida; and thinking he was moving their hearts by his mission when they were only suffering from—Prossy's complaint. (She is about to protest: he raises his hand to silence her, exclaiming) Don't try to look indignant, Candida:—

CANDIDA (interjecting). Try!

MORELL (continuing). Eugene was right. As you told me a few hours after, he is always right. He said nothing that you did not say far better yourself. He is the poet, who sees everything; and I am the poor parson, who understands nothing.

CANDIDA (remorsefully). Do you mind what is said by a foolish boy, because I said something like it again in jest?

MORELL. That foolish boy can speak with the inspiration of a child and the cunning of a serpent. He has claimed that you belong to him and not to me; and, rightly or wrongly, I have come to fear that it may be true. I will not go about tortured with doubts and suspicions. I will not live with you and keep a secret from you. I will not suffer the intolerable degradation of jealousy. We have agreed—he and I—that you shall choose between us now. I await your decision.

CANDIDA (slowly recoiling a step, her heart hardened by his rhetoric in spite of the sincere feeling behind it). Oh! I am to choose, am I? I suppose it is quite settled that I must belong to one or the other.

MORELL (firmly). Quite. You must choose definitely.

MARCHBANKS (anxiously). Morell: you don't understand. She means that she belongs to herself.

CANDIDA (turning on him). I mean that and a good deal more, Master Eugene, as you will both find out presently. And pray, my lords and masters, what have you to offer for my choice? I am up for auction, it seems. What do you bid, James?

MORELL (reproachfully). Cand— (He breaks down: his eyes and throat fill with tears: the orator becomes the wounded animal.) I can't speak—

CANDIDA (impulsively going to him). Ah, dearest—

MARCHBANKS (in wild alarm). Stop: it's not fair. You mustn't show her that you suffer, Morell. I am on the rack, too; but I am not crying.

MORELL (rallying all his forces). Yes: you are right. It is not for pity that I am bidding. (He disengages himself from Candida.)

CANDIDA (retreating, chilled). I beg your pardon, James; I did not mean to touch you. I am waiting to hear your bid.

MORELL (with proud humility). I have nothing to offer you but my strength for your defence, my honesty of purpose for your surety, my ability and industry for your livelihood, and my authority and position for your dignity. That is all it becomes a man to offer to a woman.

CANDIDA (quite quietly). And you, Eugene? What do you offer?

MARCHBANKS. My weakness! my desolation! my heart's need!

CANDIDA (impressed). That's a good bid, Eugene. Now I know how to make my choice.

She pauses and looks curiously from one to the other, as if weighing them. Morell, whose lofty confidence has changed into heartbreaking dread at Eugene's bid, loses all power of concealing his anxiety. Eugene, strung to the highest tension, does not move a muscle.

MORELL (in a suffocated voice—the appeal bursting from the depths of his anguish). Candida!

MARCHBANKS (aside, in a flash of contempt). Coward!

CANDIDA (significantly). I give myself to the weaker of the two.

Eugene divines her meaning at once: his face whitens like steel in a furnace that cannot melt it.

MORELL (bowing his head with the calm of collapse). I accept your sentence, Candida.

CANDIDA. Do you understand, Eugene?

MARCHBANKS. Oh, I feel I'm lost. He cannot bear the burden.

MORELL (incredulously, raising his head with prosaic abruptness). Do you mean, me, Candida?

CANDIDA (smiling a little). Let us sit and talk comfortably over it like three friends. (To Morell.) Sit down, dear. (Morell takes the chair from the fireside—the children's chair.) Bring me that chair, Eugene. (She indicates the easy chair. He fetches it silently, even with something like cold strength, and places it next Morell, a little behind him. She sits down. He goes to the sofa and sits there, still silent and inscrutable. When they are all settled she begins, throwing a spell of quietness on them by her calm, sane, tender tone.) You remember what you told me about yourself, Eugene: how nobody has cared for you since your old nurse died: how those clever, fashionable sisters and successful brothers of yours were your mother's and father's pets: how miserable you were at Eton: how your father is trying to starve you into returning to Oxford: how you have had to live without comfort or welcome or refuge, always lonely, and nearly always disliked and misunderstood, poor boy!

MARCHBANKS (faithful to the nobility of his lot). I had my books. I had Nature. And at last I met you.

CANDIDA. Never mind that just at present. Now I want you to look at this other boy here—MY boy—spoiled from his cradle. We go once a fortnight to see his parents. You should come with us, Eugene, and see the pictures of the hero of that household. James as a baby! the most wonderful of all babies. James holding his first school prize, won at the ripe age of eight! James as the captain of his eleven! James in his first frock coat! James under all sorts of glorious circumstances! You know how strong he is (I hope he didn't hurt you)—how clever he is—how happy! (With deepening gravity.) Ask James's mother and his three sisters what it cost to save James the trouble of doing anything but be strong and clever and happy. Ask ME what it costs to be James's mother and three sisters and wife and mother to his children all in one. Ask Prossy and Maria how troublesome the house is even when we have no visitors to help us to slice the onions. Ask the tradesmen who want to worry James and spoil his beautiful sermons who it is that puts them off. When there is money to give, he gives it: when there is money to refuse, I refuse it. I build a castle of comfort and indulgence and love for him, and stand sentinel always to keep little vulgar cares out. I make him master here, though he does not know it, and could not tell you a moment ago how it came to be so. (With sweet irony.) And when he thought I might go away with you, his only anxiety was what should become of ME! And to tempt me to stay he offered me (leaning forward to stroke his hair caressingly at each phrase) his strength for MY defence, his industry for my livelihood, his position for my dignity, his— (Relenting.) Ah, I am mixing up your beautiful sentences and spoiling them, am I not, darling? (She lays her cheek fondly against his.)

MORELL (quite overcome, kneeling beside her chair and embracing her with boyish ingenuousness). It's all true, every word. What I am you have made me with the labor of your hands and the love of your heart! You are my wife, my mother, my sisters: you are the sum of all loving care to me.

CANDIDA (in his arms, smiling, to Eugene). Am I YOUR mother and sisters to you, Eugene?

MARCHBANKS (rising with a fierce gesture of disgust). Ah, never. Out, then, into the night with me!

CANDIDA (rising quickly and intercepting him). You are not going like that, Eugene?

MARCHBANKS (with the ring of a man's voice—no longer a boy's—in the words). I know the hour when it strikes. I am impatient to do what must be done.

MORELL (rising from his knee, alarmed). Candida: don't let him do anything rash.

CANDIDA (confident, smiling at Eugene). Oh, there is no fear. He has learnt to live without happiness.

MARCHBANKS. I no longer desire happiness: life is nobler than that. Parson James: I give you my happiness with both hands: I love you because you have filled the heart of the woman I loved. Good-bye. (He goes towards the door.)

CANDIDA. One last word. (He stops, but without turning to her.) How old are you, Eugene?

MARCHBANKS. As old as the world now. This morning I was eighteen.

CANDIDA (going to him, and standing behind him with one hand caressingly on his shoulder). Eighteen! Will you, for my sake, make a little poem out of the two sentences I am going to say to you? And will you promise to repeat it to yourself whenever you think of me?

MARCHBANKS (without moving). Say the sentences.

CANDIDA. When I am thirty, she will be forty-five. When I am sixty, she will be seventy-five.

MARCHBANKS (turning to her). In a hundred years, we shall be the same age. But I have a better secret than that in my heart. Let me go now. The night outside grows impatient.

CANDIDA. Good-bye. (She takes his face in her hands; and as he divines her intention and bends his knee, she kisses his forehead. Then he flies out into the night. She turns to Morell, holding out her arms to him.) Ah, James! (They embrace. But they do not know the secret in the poet's heart.)

Hill forts in Wiltshire

Table of Contents

Barbury Castle 1
Battlesbury Camp 2
Bincknoll Castle 3
Bratton Castle 4
Bury Camp 5
Casterley Camp 6
Castle Ditches 6
Chiselbury 7
Chisenbury Camp 7
Codford Circle 8
Ebsbury 8
Fosbury Camp 9
Grovely castle 9
Knook Castle 9
Liddington Castle 12
Little Woodbury 12
Membury Camp 13
Old Sarum 13
Ringsbury Camp 15
Scratchbury Camp 15
Sidbury Hill, Wiltshire 20
Vespasian's Camp 21
Whitesheet Hill 22
Yarnbury Castle 22

Preface

Each chapter in this book ends with a URL to a hyperlinked online version. Use the online version to access related pages, websites, footnotes, tables, color photos, updates, or to see the chapter's contributors. Click the edit link to suggest changes. Please type the URL exactly as it appears. If you change the URL's capitalization, for example, it may not work.

Purchase of this book entitles you to a free trial membership in the publisher's book club at www.booksllc.net. (Time limited offer.) Simply enter the barcode number from the back cover onto the membership form on our home page. The book club entitles you to select from millions of books at no additional charge, including a PDF copy of this and related books to read on the go. Simply enter the title or subject onto the search form to find them.

If you have any questions, could you please be so kind as to consult our Frequently Asked Questions page at www.booksllc.net/faqs.cfm? You are also welcome to contact us there.

Publisher: Books LLC, Wiki Series, Memphis, TN, USA, 2013.

Barbury Castle

Barbury Castle

Steep earthworks (with cowslips) looking northwards

Shown within Wiltshire

Location	Wiltshire
Region	GB
Coordinates	
Type	landmark
Area	12 acres (4.9 ha)
History	
Periods	Iron Age
Site notes	
Public access	yes, The Ridgeway

Barbury Castle is an Iron Age hill fort situated in Wiltshire, England. It is one of several such forts found along the ancient Ridgeway route. The site, which lies within the Wessex Downs Area of Outstanding Natural Beauty, has been managed as a country park by Swindon Borough Council since 1971. It is situated on Barbury Hill, a local vantage point, which, under ideal weather conditions, commands a view across to the Cotswolds and the River Severn. It has two deep defensive ditches and ramparts. The Old Ridgeway runs close by and the modern Ridgeway crosses through the castle. In the surrounding area are to be found round barrows, Celtic field systems and 18th-19th Century flint workings.

History

The site was first occupied some 2500 years ago, and was then in use during the Roman occupation of the area. Archaeological investigations at Barbury have shown evidence of a number of buildings, indicating a village or military garrison at this time.

In the 6th century the site became part of the Saxon kingdom of Wessex following the defeat of the Romano-British at the Battle of Beranburgh, Beran Byrig or Beranbyrig in AD 556, the site of which is just north of the castle.

The Iron Age house under construction - July 2006.

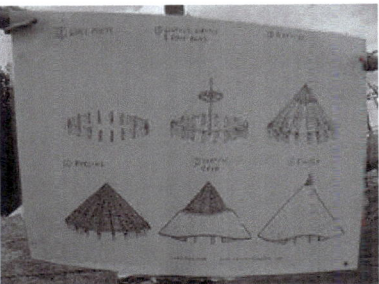

Plans of the Iron Age house.

Centuries later the area was a favourite haunt of the 19th century writer Richard Jefferies, who lived an hour's walk away at Coate.

In World War II the War Ministry appropriated the site for US Army Air Force anti-aircraft guns; the bases for these are apparently visible as hollows around the edge of the fort interior.

In 1996 a geophysical survey revealed traces of 40 hut circles inside the castle. A reconstruction of an Iron Age roundhouse was built on the site in 2006 but was sacked by vandals in October 2008.

Location

Barbury Castle is at grid reference SU149762, about 5 miles (8 km) south of Swindon and the M4, on the northern edge of the Marlborough Downs within the North Wessex Downs Area of Outstanding Natural Beauty. Other than a couple of nearby farms, there is no current settlement near the site.

Looking northwards over Swindon

Looking westwards towards the River Severn

By road the site can only approached by a single road ascending the scarp slope of the downs from midway along the B4005 between Wroughton and Chiseldon. More options are available by foot or horseback, including the Ridgeway, which runs east – west along the edge of the downs, and a byway south across the downs to Marlborough.

Nearby towns and cities: Swindon, Marlborough

Nearby villages: Wroughton, Chiseldon

Source http://en.wikipedia.org/wiki/Barbury_Castle

Battlesbury Camp

Battlesbury Camp

Iron age earth walls and ditch, at the eastern edge of Battlesbury Hillfort

Shown within Wiltshire

Location	Wiltshire
Coordinates	
Area	23.5 acres
History	
Periods	Bronze Age, Iron Age
Site notes	
Excavation dates	yes
Condition	good
Public access	yes

Battlesbury Camp is the site of an Iron Age bivallate hillfort on Battlesbury Hill in Wiltshire in South West England. Excavations and surveys at the site have uncovered various finds and archaeological data.

Background

Hill forts developed in the Late Bronze and Early Iron Age, roughly the start of the first millennium BC. The reason for their emergence in Britain, and their purpose, has been a subject of debate. It has been argued that they could have been military sites constructed in response to invasion from continental Europe, sites built by invaders, or a military reaction to social tensions caused by an increasing population and consequent pressure on agriculture. The dominant view since the 1960s has been that the increasing use of iron led to social changes in Britain. Deposits of iron ore were located in different places to the tin and copper ore necessary to make bronze, and as a result trading patterns shifted and the old elites lost their economic and social status. Power passed into the hands of a new group of people. Archaeologist Barry Cunliffe believes that population increase still played a role and has stated "[the forts] provided defensive possibilities for the community at those times when the stress [of an increasing population] burst out into open warfare. But I wouldn't see them as having been built because there was a state of war. They would be functional as defensive strongholds when there were tensions and undoubtedly some of them were attacked and destroyed, but this was not the only, or even the most significant, factor in their construction".

Description

Battlesbury occupies the summit of an irregular point of down, with its defences following the natural contours of the hill, and being by nature of the site almost inaccessible on the west and northeast sides. It has triple ditches and ramparts for the most part, with double on the southeast side. The site encloses 23.5 acres in all. There are entrances at the northwest and northwest corners.

Pits found within the fortifications contained late Iron Age pottery, the hub of a chariot wheel, an iron carpenter's saw, a latch-lifter for a hut door, querns, whetstones, sling stones, and animal bones. These all indicate a permanent

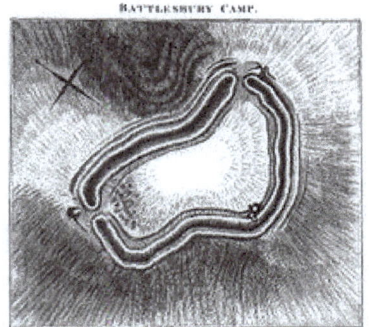

Pencil sketch of Battlesbury Camp, from *The Ancient History of Wiltshire* by Sir Richard Colt Hoare, 1810

occupation and date from the 1st century BC. Unfortunately it is suspected that the hills inhabitants came to a violent end, due to the many graves containing men, women and children outside of the northwest entrance. It can only be guessed at whether Roman legions put people to the sword, or if this was the result of intertribal warfare sometime before the Roman conquest.

The southwest area of the hill fort is apparently built over and around preceding Bronze Age burial mounds or tumuli. Part of the inner ditch is occupied by a large circular barrow, which was excavated, but was found empty. A few feet further to the west are two other barrows, over which the great inner rampart passes; these on opening, proved to be sepulchral: in the largest was found a cist containing burned human bones at the depth of two feet; and in the smallest, two skeletons were found, lying from south to north, the head of the smallest reclining on the breast of the other. On the breast of the largest skeleton there was a small ring or bead of stone, which was probably worn as an amulet.

Later excavations and surveys adjacent to Battlesbury Camp hillfort in 1998 have also uncovered late Bronze Age to middle Iron Age settlement activity including for ditches, roundhouses, four-post structures and numerous pits. Some of the pits contained human burials, and other deposits of artifacts and animal bones which appear to have been formally placed.

Location

The site is located at grid reference ST898455, to the east of the town of Warminster, in the county of Wiltshire. The hill has a summit of 208m AOD, and is marked by an Ordnance Survey Triangulation station. Nearby to the southeast lies the hillfort of Scratchbury Camp on Scratchbury hill. The site and surrounding downs are easily accessible by public footpath, however care must be taken not to stray into the Military Firing ranges of Salisbury Plain immediately to the northeast.

Source http://en.wikipedia.org/wiki/Battlesbury_Camp

Bincknoll Castle

Bincknoll Castle, Wiltshire

Shown within Wiltshire

Alternate name	Bincknoll Camp
Location	Wiltshire
Coordinates	
Area	23.5 acres
History	
Periods	Bronze Age, Iron Age
Site notes	
Condition	good
Public access	yes

Bincknoll Castle' or **Bincknoll Camp**, is the site of an Iron Age univallate hillfort located in Wiltshire. The site lies on the end of a triangular promentary on the escarpment beneath the Ridgeway to the South. The steeply contoured sides offer excellent natural defences with only the level lands to the south offering easy access. Pronounced 'Bynol' Castle, the ironage earthworks were reinforced by a later Norman motte and bailey castle of considerable natural strength. It is likely that Gilbert of Breteuil, who after the Norman conquest acquired a block of manors centred on Broad Hinton, built the castle to oversee them. The 'motte', now severely mutilated by later quarrying, measures approximately 52 metres in diameter by 3 metres high, and its ditch is 2.3 metres deep. The inner enclosure has a bank and ditch 3.4 metres high dividing it from the outer enclosure, with a causeway entrance. The earthworks of the now deserted hamlet of Bincknoll, which grew up outside the castle, may be discerned in Bincknoll Dip, sloping away to the north.

Location

The site is located at grid reference SU107793, to the west of the village of Wroughton, and to the north of the village of Broad Hinton in the county of Wiltshire. Barbury Castle hill fort is about 3.5 miles away to the South-East. The site has a summit of 195m AOD, and is easily accessible from the White Horse trail, and other public footpaths.

Source http://en.wikipedia.org/wiki/Bincknoll_Castle

Bratton Castle

Bratton Castle

Shown within Wiltshire

Alternate name	Bratton Camp
Location	Wiltshire
Coordinates	
Area	25 acres (10 ha)
History	
Periods	Bronze Age, Iron Age
Site notes	
Excavation dates	yes
Archaeologists	William Cunnington
	Sir Richard Colt Hoare
	Jeffery Whittaker
Condition	good
Ownership	English Heritage
Public access	yes
Website	http://www.english-herit org.uk/daysout/propertie bratton-camp-and-white-

Bratton Castle (also known as **Bratton Camp**) is a bivallate Iron Age hillfort on Bratton Down, at the western edge of the Salisbury Plain escarpment. The hillfort comprises two circuits of ditch and bank which together enclose a pentagonal area of 9.3 hectares (23 acres).

The Westbury White Horse, a hill figure first documented in 1742, lies on the west side of the hillfort.

Background

Hill forts developed in the Late Bronze and Early Iron Age, roughly the start of the first millennium BC. The reason for their emergence in Britain, and their purpose, has been a subject of debate. It has been argued that they could have been military sites constructed in response to invasion from continental Europe, sites built by invaders, or a military reaction to social tensions caused by an increasing population and consequent pressure on agriculture. The dominant view since the 1960s has been that the increasing use of iron led to social changes in Britain. Deposits of iron ore were located in different places to the tin and copper ore necessary to make bronze, and as a result trading patterns shifted and the old elites lost their economic and social status. Power passed into the hands of a new group of people. Archaeologist Barry Cunliffe believes that population increase still played a role and has stated "[the forts] provided defensive possibilities for the community at those times when the stress [of an increasing population] burst out into open warfare. But I wouldn't see them as having been built because there was a state of war. They would be functional as defensive strongholds when there were tensions and undoubtedly some of them were attacked and destroyed, but this was not the only, or even the most significant, factor in their construction".

Description

The short west side and the long north side occupy the crest of steep escarpment slopes and the ditches are stepped one above the other, the rampart slopes rising 5 metres (16 ft) and 6 metres (20 ft) above the base of the ditches. The defences here span a total width of 30 metres (98 ft). The south side of the hillfort and the southern half of the east side cross Bratton Down and here the twin ramparts are of roughly equal height and 30 metres (98 ft) in width. The northern half of the east side crosses the head of a re-entrant valley where the outer rampart and ditch have been largely destroyed by quarrying or landslips and the construction of a farm track. The short north east side straddles a narrow steep-sided ridge up which runs the Port Way. This passes through a possible original entrance, at which point the two ramparts have separated to form a small annexe, the outer ditch of which has, in places, been removed

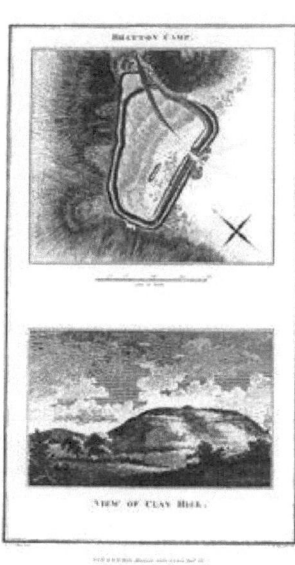

Pencil sketches of Bratton Camp, from *The Ancient History of Wiltshire* by Sir Richard Colt Hoare

by quarrying. Quarrying has, in the past, also taken place within parts of the interior of the fort.

Archaeology

The hillfort was one of the sites excavated by Jeffery Whittaker prior to 1775, which is thought to have been one of the earliest archaeological excavations to have taken place in Wiltshire. The excavation was poorly documented but it is believed that Roman and Saxon coins were found within the vicinity of the fort. Later excavations were carried out by William Cunnington and Sir Richard Colt Hoare. Notably three barrows within and around the castle were excavated and recorded

Bratton G1

A Long Barrow, within which was found two primary cremations on a platform with a pile of pebble stones and one chalk bead covered with 'vegetable earth', intermixed with pottery and animal bones at four and five feet deep. Three secondary inhumations were found near the top.

Bratton G2

A Bowl barrow containing two cremation urns, the one placed within the other, and an interment of burnt bones. The large urn was broken in pieces; the small one, containing about three pints was better preserved and is contained within the Wiltshire Heritage Museum. It is described as particular in its shape, having a perforated and projecting handle.

Bratton G8a

A small round barrow less than one foot high, contained a circular cist with a crouched skeleton, but no relics. The skull is at Cambridge Museum.

Location

The site is located at grid reference ST90125164, to the southwest of the village and parish of Bratton, in the county of Wiltshire. The hill has a summit of 225 m (738 ft) AOD. The site and surrounding downs are easily accessible by public footpath.

Source http://en.wikipedia.org/wiki/Bratton_Castle

The Memorial to the Battle of Ethandun is a sarson stone standing in a corner of the public recreation area adjacent to Bratton Castle

Bury Camp

Bury Camp	
Shown within Wiltshire	
Alternate name	Bury Wood Camp, or North Wood
Location	Wiltshire
Coordinates	
History	
Periods	Iron Age
Site notes	
Excavation dates	yes
Archaeologists	Dr Denis Grant-King
Condition	good
Public access	yes

Bury Camp is the site of an Iron Age multivallate hillfort located in Wiltshire. It is located on a triangular promontory of Colerne Down at the southern edge of the Cotswold Hills between two spurs of a river valley. The enclosed area approximately 9.2ha, and is surrounded by a ditch 4m wide and up to 1m deep, and an outer rampart up to 1.5m high on the east and northwestern sides and up to 2m high on the southwestern side, across the neck of the promontory.

The contours of the land provide excellent natural defences to the north and east sides. On the south western side, where there are no natural defences, there is a further ditch 4m wide and 1m deep and an outer rampart up to 2m high and 3m wide. These are crossed by many causeways, which could be interpreted as an indication that the construction of the monument was never fully completed. The entrance in the middle of the south western side is thought to be of modern origin. At the north eastern corner the inner bank turns inwards to form a funnel shaped entrance leading to a hollow way running down the steep scarp into the valley below. Another entrance about a quarter of the way along the north western side also consists of inward turning ramparts forming a funnel shaped entrance.

A small enclosure within the camp is visible on aerial photographs. It is circular, 72m in diameter, with a bank and an outer ditch. The site is a scheduled national monument no.28993.

Excavations carried out under Dr Denis Grant-King, from 1959 onwards, turned over some good examples of Iron Age drystone walling, and has found remains of a much earlier structure that existed at the north east entrance, indicated by drystone revetments within the northern rampart. In a second stage the entrance was remodelled and widened. At the north west entrance, four staggered post holes were uncovered as well as a cylindrical cavity 0.66m deep, interpreted as a gate post hole.

The general history of the fort, beginning with its initial building, can be dated to about 350 BC, however various Neolithic and Mesolithic flint tools were found, indicating a much earlier use. Flint artefacts including scrapers, cores and flakes were found within the camp. Rotary and saddle querns were also found, along with a possible axe polishing stone. In 1960, 175 shards of pottery were recovered. All except one was plain coarse ware without a trace of decoration.

Of organic remains, only two fragments of human bones were found, whereas between 400 and 500 animal bone fragments were found. This included for typical domestic animals such as sheep, goats, cattle, pigs, horses and dogs. Six specimens were of very large birds, probably swans or geese. Deer, fox, rabbit and vole bones were also found. The relative rarity of anything but domestic animals may suggest that the camp was based on stock keeping and that it was unlikely that hunting played a large part of the food economy of the camp.

Casterley Camp

Casterley Camp

Casterley Camp

Shown within Wiltshire

Location	Wiltshire
Coordinates	
History	
Periods	Iron Age
Site notes	
Public access	yes

Casterley Camp is the site of an Iron Age univallate hillfort located in Wiltshire. The site comprises a large Iron Age/Romano-British enclosure, possibly non-defensive in function, and incomplete. The site was partially excavated in the 19th century.

Location
The site is located at grid reference ST818740, to the south of the village of North Wraxall, in the county of Wiltshire. The site has a height of 145m AOD. The Fosseway Roman road passes very close by to the west.

Source http://en.wikipedia.org/wiki/Bury_Camp

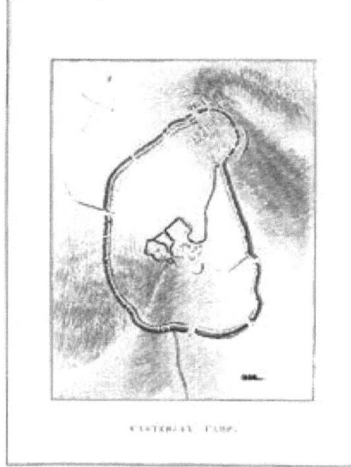

Pencil sketch of Castlerley camp by Sir Richard Colt-Hoare, 1810, *The Ancient History of Wiltshire*

Three apparently related enclosures are identified situated within the site of Casterley Camp. Stock control and religious functions have been attributed to the enclosures. The excavations uncoverred Samian, New Forest and Coarse ware, coins, bronze earpicks, pins and tweezers, a stamp and knives, nails etc. There is also an Iron Age/Romano-British trackway on the west side of Casterley Camp, with traces of an earth banks on both sides. The site is a scheduled monument no.10037

Location
The site is located at grid reference SU115535, to the southwest of the small village of Upavon, in the county of Wiltshire. The site lies at a level of between 155m and 175m AOD. There are public footpaths and bridleways to the north and west of the site. The Salisbury Plain firing ranges lie immediately to the west.

The smaller Iron Age hill fort of Chisenbury Camp lies close by to the east.

Source http://en.wikipedia.org/wiki/Casterley_Camp

Castle Ditches

Castle Ditches

Woods around Castle Ditches

Alternate name	Spelsbury
Location	Wiltshire
Coordinates	

Shown within Wiltshire

Area	24 acres
History	
Periods	Iron Age
Site notes	
Public access	no

Castle Ditches is the site of an Iron Age trivallate hillfort located in Wiltshire. It is probable that its ancient name was *Spelsbury*. Its shape is roughly triangular, and follows the contours of the small hill upon which it sits. The earthworks comprise triple row of ramparts and ditches, which are covered on three sides with woodland. There is a large entrance towards the south-east, where there is the shallowest incline of the hill; but there is also a narrow slit on the opposite side. The area within the site encompasses nearly 24 acres, and the greatest height of the ramparts is about forty feet.

Chiselbury

Chiselbury

Chiselbury

Shown within Wiltshire

Location	Wiltshire
Coordinates	
Area	10.5 acres
History	
Periods	Iron Age
Site notes	
Public access	yes

Chiselbury is the site of an Iron Age univallate hillfort located in Wiltshire. The hillfort is sub-circular in plan, and encloses an area of approximately 10.5 acres. It is defined by an earthen rampart up to 3.6m in height and an external ditch, up to a maximum of 1.6m in depth. A gap in the southeastern side of the rampart, and a corresponding causeway across the ditch, is thought to be the original entrance and is associated with a small 'D' shaped embanked enclosure, which is apparently visible on aerial photographs. Although the enclosure has subsequently been degraded by ploughing, it is still apparent as a series of low earthworks.

Limited archaeological investigation of the interior of the hillfort in the early 20th century failed to find any direct traces of occupation. However, outside of the fort some Iron Age pottery and a lead spindle whorl were found. In addition, two Roman coins, one of which dated to the reign of Emperor Constantine I, were said to have been found within the central area. An Iron Age sword and scabbard were also found on the nearby trackway which runs along the ridge top.

The hillfort is abutted on both its northern and southern sides by embanked ditches or cross dykes. Their precise function is unknown but the manner in which they cut the ridge suggests that they were intended to prevent movement along it. The Northern Cross dyke, 90 metres (300 ft) in length, ran from the ditch of the hillfort across the top of the ridge before continuing part way down its northern slopes. Although visible in 1928, the section between the hillfort and the edge of the ridge has subsequently been infilled by ploughing, but survives as a buried feature. The Southern Cross dyke, which survives as a discontinuous series of banks and ditches, (sections of which are filled in but survive as buried features) is a total of 180 metres (590 ft) in length. It travels roughly south-southeast from the 'D' shaped enclosure, down the southern slope of the ridge, and into the base of a valley.

An aerial photograph from 1928 clearly shows the southern cross dyke continuing as a buried feature beneath a trackway which runs along the ridge top, indicating that the trackway came into use after the cross dyke was constructed. An Anglo-Saxon charter also mentions 'the ridgeway' suggesting that the trackway was in use by at least the early medieval period. Referred to as the 'Ten Mile Course' by Dr. Stukeley in 1776, in the medieval and post-medieval periods the trackway was the main route from Wilton to Shaftesbury. By the 18th century it had become a turnpike road, and a map dated to 1773 depicts a toll house immediately to the south of it. The remains of the former toll house structure are visible today as a series of earthworks representing a building platform with a small enclosure immediately to its east.

The site is a scheduled national monument no.1020262.

Today, the site is also famous for the Fovant Badges, which are a number of regimental badges cut into the chalk of the hill on its northern flank. These were created by soldiers garrisoned near Fovant during the First World War, and are clearly visible from the A30 which runs through the village.

Location

The site is located at grid reference SU018281, to the southeast of the small village of Fovant, in the county of Wiltshire. The hill has a summit of 201m AOD. There are public footpaths and bridleways to the east and south of the site.

Source http://en.wikipedia.org/wiki/Chiselbury

Location

The site is located at grid reference ST964282, to the southeast of the small town of Tisbury, in the county of Wiltshire. The hill has a summit of 193m AOD. The River Nadder flows close by to the north of the site. There are public footpaths surrounding all parts of the site, but the land is privately owned.

Source http://en.wikipedia.org/wiki/Castle_Ditches

Chisenbury Camp

Chisenbury Camp

possibly Cissanbyrig

Location	Wiltshire
Coordinates	
History	
Periods	Iron Age
Site notes	
Public access	no

Shown within Wiltshire

Chisenbury Camp is the site of an Iron Age univallate hillfort located in Wiltshire. The site comprises a small circular 5 acre enclosure that was unfortunately levelled in 1931. A post was part excavated while being demolished. The site was partially excavated in the 19th century and there were finds of ceramics, worked stone, worked animal bone and remains of human burial.

The site currently lies within the bounds of a small grassstrip airfield, *Upavon Airfield*, and is run through by the perimeter access road on the southern side of the field.

Location

The site is located at grid reference SU15195387, to the southeast of the small village of Upavon, in the county of Wiltshire. The site lies at a level of approximately 160mAOD.

The larger Iron Age hill fort of Casterley Camp lies close by to the west. There are also a number of other Iron Age earthworks in the area, including for **Lidbury Camp**. (scheduled monument no.10043) to the southeast, but this is too small to be a hill fort or plateau fort, measuring just 90m across. There are also numerous ditches, barrows, trackways, field systems, and tumuli in the area.

Source http://en.wikipedia.org/wiki/Chisenbury_Camp

Codford Circle

Codford Circle

Shown within Wiltshire

Alternate name	Oldbury Camp, Wilsbury Ring, Woldsbury
Location	Wiltshire
Region	Southern England
Coordinates	
Type	Hilltop enclosure or possible hillfort
Area	3.6 ha (8.9 acres)
Height	188 m (617 ft)
History	
Material	Chalk
Periods	possible Neolithic
Site notes	
Archaeologists	Sir Richard Colt Hoare, W.F.Cunnington,

Codford Circle, also known as **Wilsbury Ring**, and **Woldsbury**, and possibly **Oldbury Camp**, is a neolithic hill top enclosure or possible hillfort located on the summit of Codford Hill, a chalk promontory of Salisbury Plain, near to the village and civil parish of Codford, in Wiltshire.

The site is oval in plan and approximately of 3.6 ha (8.9 acres) and is surrounded by a bank 6.5 metres (21 ft) wide and up to 1.6 m (5.2 ft) high. It is surrounded by a ditch 5 metres (16 ft) wide and up to 0.5 metres (1.6 ft) deep, although an area on the south eastern edge has been reduced by ploughing. Aerial photography shows signs of an inner ditch, possibly signs of a former palisade fence, and entrances on the east and west sides. The entrances on the southeast and northwest sides are later in origin.

There is no archaeological evidence for occupation, and the slight nature of the earthworks have been interpreted as being defensively weak, therefore the site is currently interpretted as an enclosure of an unknown but ancient date.

Source http://en.wikipedia.org/wiki/Codford_Circle

Ebsbury

Ebsbury

The northern flank of Ebsbury Hill with strip lynchets visible

Shown within Wiltshire

Alternate name	Grovely Earthworks
Location	Wiltshire
Region	Southern England
Coordinates	
Type	possible hillfort
History	
Periods	Iron Age
Site notes	
Excavation dates	1906
Archaeologists	SW Doughty

The site of **Ebsbury** includes the remains of an Iron Age enclosed settlement, field system and possible hillfort, and a Romano-British enclosed settlement, located in the parish of Barford St Martin, in Wiltshire.

The site occupies the spur of a downland hill with the possible hillfort enclosure measuring approximately 700 m (770 yd) by 400 m (440 yd), inside of which lie the remains of a field system with two further smaller oval enclosures and one triangular enclosure. To the north and east sides of the site the contours of the hill have been reinforced by multiple banks. The site of an Iron Age settlement lies to the eastern end of the site.

The site was subject to archaeological surveys and excavations in 1906 by S.W. Doughty. Finds include a Neolithic perforated mace-head and two Roman coin hoards. The latter were found buried in two earthenware pots; the coins date from between AD 337 and AD 408, and were found with the remains of a glass vessel, and six silver rings.

Location
The site is located at grid reference SU061354, just to the west of the village of Great Wishford. The hill has a summit of 175 m (574 ft) AOD. Nearby to the west lies the site of Grovely castle, and to the south, the largest forest in Wiltshire, Grovely Wood.

Source http://en.wikipedia.org/wiki/Ebsbury

Fosbury Camp

Fosbury Camp

Fosbury Camp, looking along the inner wall of the Iron Age hillfort towards Oakhill Wood

Shown within Wiltshire

Alternate name	Haydon Hill Castle
Location	Wiltshire
Coordinates	
Area	26 acres (11 ha)
History	
Periods	Iron Age
Site notes	
Public access	yes

Fosbury Camp, is the site of an Iron Age bivallate hillfort located in Wiltshire. The site is oval in shape, and approximately 26 acres in area

The site is a scheduled national monument number WI162. The fort sits atop *Knolls Down* and is excellently defended to the south, south west, and east, from the very steeply sloped topology. To the north the land is less steep, and is mostly bounded by *Oakhill Wood*. To the west the ground rises to the true summit of *Haydown Hill*. In the eastern side of the camp there lies a pond, perhaps an original feature of the neolithic site.

Location
The site is located at grid reference SU319565, south of the village and civil parish of Fosbury in Wiltshire, and is near the towns of Marlborough and Hungerford. It lies at a height of 254m AOD, slightly below the summit of the hill at 258m AOD. The site is easily accessed by public footpaths running to the north of the site, and the borders of *Oakhill Wood*.

Source http://en.wikipedia.org/wiki/Fosbury_Camp

Grovely castle

Grovely castle

Shown within Wiltshire

Location	Wiltshire
Region	Southern England
Coordinates	
Type	possible hillfort
Area	13 acres (5.3 ha)
History	
Periods	Iron Age
Site notes	
Archaeologists	P.F.Ewence
	Grinsell

Grovely castle is the site of an Iron Age univallate hill-fort in the Parish of Steeple Langford, in Wiltshire. The remaining ramparts stand approximately 3.2 m (10 ft) high, with 1.5 m (4.9 ft) deep ditches, although ploughing has damaged the earthworks in some parts of the site. Excavations have uncovered the remains of five human skeletons within the ramparts. Entrances are located in the southwest and northeast corners of the hillfort. A circular enclosure of 35 to 40 m (115 to 130 ft) is evident in aerial photographs of the hillfort interior. There is also a later bank and ditch which runs through the hillfort from south-west to north-east, and is probably part of an extensive surrounding Celtic field system.

Location
The site is located at grid reference SU048357, to the south of the village of Little Langford. The site has a summit of 156 m (512 ft) AOD. Nearby to the east lies the Iron Age site of Ebsbury, and to the south, the largest forest in Wiltshire, Grovely Wood.

Source http://en.wikipedia.org/wiki/Grovely_castle

Knook Castle

Knook Castle

Knook Castle

Shown within Wiltshire

Location	Wiltshire
Region	Southern England
Coordinates	
Type	sub-rectangular univallate hillfort
Area	1.75 hectares (4.3 acres)
History	
Material	Chalk
Periods	Iron Age
Site notes	
Archaeologists	Sir Richard Colt Hoare,
	W.F.Cunnington,
	Petrie,
	Grinsell
Public access	footpaths

Knook Castle is the site of an Iron Age univallate hillfort located on Knook Downs, near the village and of Knook in Wiltshire, but falls within the civil parsih of the nearby village of Upton Lovell. It has also been interpreted as a defensive cattle enclosure associated with nearby Romano-British settlements. It is roughly rectangular in plan with a single entrance on the south/southeast side, but with a later break in the wall on the western side.

John Marius Wilson's *Imperial Gazetteer of England and Wales* (1870–1872) described Knook Castle as follows:

Knook Castle is an ancient single ditched entrenchment, of about 2 acres; is supposed to have been originally a British village, and afterwards a Roman summer camp; and has yielded Roman coins. Traces of another ancient British village are to the N. "The site of these villages," says Sir R.Hoare, "is decidedly marked by great cavities and a black soil; and the attentive eye may easily trace out the lines of houses and the streets, or rather the hollow ways, conducting to them. Numerous tumuli and barrows are in the neighbourhood."

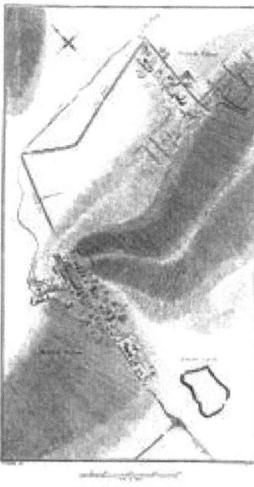

A pencil sketch of Knook Castle and the adjacent Romano-British settlements of Knook Down East and Knook Down West, from *The Ancient History of Wiltshire*, by Sir Richard Colt-Hoare, 1810.

The site and surrounding downs are easily accessible by public footpath, with the *Imber Range perimeter path* running east to west immediately to the north of the site. Further to the north lies the military firing ranges of Salisbury Plain.

Romano British Settlements

Nearby, some 300m to the north of the hillfort, and slightly further to the north east, are the sites of two Romano British settlements of *Knook Down East* and *Knook Down West*. They lie approximately 600m apart and are linked by an earlier linear ditch or hollow way.

Knook Down East covers approximately 4 ha (9.9 acres) and is well preserved around a central trackway feature that runs north to south, with 11no. surrounding scooped platforms and enclosures. **Knook Down West** covers approximately 11 ha (27 acres) and may comprise two distinct settlements. The

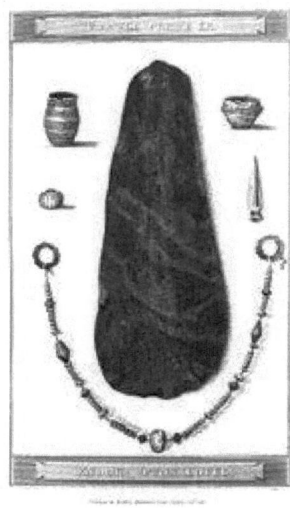

A pencil sketch showing findings from tumuli within Knook and Upton Lovell parishes, from *The Ancient History of Wiltshire*, by Sir Richard Colt-Hoare, 1810

northern side of the site has a central area off of which are five trackways that serve a number of enclosures. On the southern side of the site are three enclosures. Between the two areas lies a field system, with the north and south sides linked by a trackway, which follows the line of a pre-Roman linear ditch.

Finds at the sites and the surrounding areas date predominantly from the 2nd to 4th centuries AD, and include for bones, bracelets, nails, door-furniture, Roman coins, stone flooring, hearths with painted stucco and brick, and burial remains found with a basalt axe.

Possible associated landscape featues also include for extensive surrounding field systems, boundary earthworks, ponds, two corn-drying kilns, and the outline of a possible small amphiteatre, or circus.

Archaeology

Excavations at the hillfort and the surrounding areas have revealed many items from Neolithic, Bronze Age, Iron Age and Romano British periods. Most of the various finds discovered are now preserved at the Wiltshire Heritage Museum in Devizes.

Most recently in the 1950s, the archaeologist Leslie Grinsell has reviewed and indexed the site and surrounding features. Earlier excavations by Sir Richard Colt Hoare and William Cunnington in the 1800s revealed most of the various finds and interments. However, as the three-age system had not yet been introduced, they were unable to date their finds and therefore were at a disadvantage when trying to interpret them. The following table includes for details of the nearby surrounding tumuli, barrows, and other ancient features. The tumuli and barrows are referenced by Grinsells reference system which uses the original parish name. Only the *Knook* referenced sites are shown here although there are many other Grinsell referenced tumuli also to be found nearby which fall into the adjacent parishes of *Chitterne, Codford,* and *Heytesbury*; some of which form part of the Aston Valley Barrow Cemetery, some 2000m to the southeast of the hillfort.

Name/ reference	Location	Type	Size
Knook 1 (Grinsell)	grid reference ST93694128	Bowl barrow	50 (46 wi… 3 f 91
Knook 1a (Grinsell)	grid reference ST95464431	Bowl barrow	15 (14 wi… 75 23
Knook Barrow,	grid reference ST95614461	Long Barrow	100 (30 lon…
Knook 2 (Grinsell)			50 (15 wi… 6 f 8 n
Knook 3 (Grinsell)	grid reference ST95604457, 30m to the west of Knook Long barrow (ST 94 SE 18).	Bowl Barrow	12 (39 wi… 8 n 6 f
Knook 4 (Grinsell)	grid reference ST96564549	Bowl Barrow	17 (16 wi… 5 f 76
Knook 4a & 4b (Grinsell)	grid reference ST965455	Bowl Barrows	No rer…
Knock 5 (Grinsell)	grid reference ST96754625	Long Barrow	No rer… des 19… wa app 78 (24 lon 3 f 91
Knock 5b (Grinsell)	grid reference ST94804375	Bowl Barrow	No rer…
Monument no.211561	grid reference ST94804375	Earthwork	
Monument no.867365	grid reference ST96334459	Ring ditch	45 14 16…
Monument no.867362	grid reference ST959447	Neolithic flat grave	
Monument no.887361	grid reference ST9544	Complex of boundary earthworks	

Liddington Castle

Liddington Castle

Liddington Castle, locally called **Liddington Camp**, is a late Bronze Age and early Iron Age hill fort in the English county of Wiltshire.

It is sited on a commanding high points close to The Ridgeway and covers an area of 3ha. Liddington Castle was one of the earliest hill forts in Britain, with first occupation dating to the seventh century BC. The earthworks consist of a relatively simple oval bank of timber and earth fronted by a ditch, with opposing causewayed entrances on the east and west sides. The western entrance was later blocked off and the eastern one may have been lined with sarsen stones. A palisade of wooden posts may have lined the top of the bank. During a later phase the bank and ditch were improved and a rampart of dumped chalk, excavated from the enlarged ditch, increased the height of the bank.

Excavation within the hill fort revealed a large pit 1.5m in diameter and at least 2.4m deep. The bottom of the feature was not reached and it was interpreted by the archaeologists who dug it as a ritual shaft. Similar shafts have been recorded at Wapley Hill in Herefordshire and Cadbury Castle in Devon. Finds of pottery suggest Liddington Castle was abandoned during the fifth century BC, with perhaps some later reoccupation during the Roman period.

Earthworks at Liddington Castle

Liddington Castle is sometimes suggested as a possible site of Mount Badon and thus the location of the late fifth century AD Battle of Mount Badon in Arthurian myth. There is, however, no archaeological evidence to indicate activity during this later period.

Liddington Castle was the favourite haunt of local writer of natural history and rural life, Richard Jefferies, who spent much of his spare time walking through the wide chalk expanses of the Marlborough Downs. It was on this summit that he relates in The Story of My Heart that his unusual sensitivity to nature began to induce in him a powerful inner awakening - a desire for a larger existence or reality.

Unlike the neighbouring castles of Uffington and Barbury, Liddington Castle is relatively unvisited in spite of being a clearly visible landmark to the millions who pass along the M4 motorway south of Swindon. While accessible by a permissive footpath and less than a mile from The Ridgeway it is not served by a car park, hence any visitor will usually find themselves quite alone to enjoy its secluded atmosphere.

Liddington Castle, at 277 metres (909 ft), is the highest point in the Borough of Swindon

Source http://en.wikipedia.org/wiki/Liddington_Castle

Little Woodbury

Little Woodbury is the name of an important Iron Age archaeological site near Salisbury in the English county of Wiltshire.

It was partially excavated between 1938 and 1939 by Gerhard Bersu, a German archaeologist who introduced the revolutionary approaches he had developed in continental Europe before being driven to Britain by the Nazis. He was commissioned by the Prehistoric Society to excavate the site in order to improve knowledge of early British settlement sites which were until then poorly understood.

A settlement had been identified at the site through aerial archaeology by OGS Crawford almost 20 years previously. He had seen a circular enclosure as a cropmark and it was identified for further excavation as a possible source of information on everyday prehistoric Britain.

Bersu dug a network of parallel

trenches, one after the other across the site. Through this methodology, he was able to identify a large roundhouse and several other domestic features. The postholes of the roundhouse enabled Bersu to argue that these structures were the common domestic building type of the Iron Age, prior to his work it was thought that people lived in holes in the ground. Through Bersu's identification of animal bone and cereal grains, he convinced other archaeologists to re-evaluate these large holes they found as storage pits.

When war broke out in 1939, work stopped and Bersu was interned on the Isle of Man. He never returned to the site and post-excavation work was never fully completed. The results from Little Woodbury however served to influence generations of archaeologists to take an interest in the day-to-day life of ancient peoples and the roundhouse has become a regular feature in interpreting prehistoric sites.

Source http://en.wikipedia.org/wiki/Little_Woodbury

Membury Camp

Membury Camp

Shown within Wiltshire

Alternate name	Membury Fort
Location	Wiltshire
Coordinates	
Area	14 hectares
Height	200m
History	
Periods	Iron Age
Site notes	
Public access	yes

Membury Camp, or **Membury Fort**, is the site of an Iron Age hillfort located on the borders of Wiltshire and Berkshire, (the county line divides the site in two, although the majority of the site lies within Wiltshire). The site encompasses 14 hectares, and is situated in the south-western corner of a small plateau. The circular earthworks are completely shrouded in trees and inside the walls it is mostly arable farmland. To the northeast, in the Berkshire segment, the camp is totally wooded by a small copse, *Walls Copse*, which covers a quarter of the site. To the north and east the adjoining ground is flat, but to the south and west it falls away steeply, providing a natural defence. The camp consists of a single ditch with banks on either side and encloses and area measuring 390m by 490m. A gap in the east with inturning flanks is probably an original entrance though it is mutilated and overgrown. Other gaps in the banks appear to be more modern. A possible hut circle is visible as a cropmark situated at the south end of the hillfort. The east side of the earthwork has been partly destroyed by the construction of a wartime airfield, RAF Membury. The site has not been excavated but a number of prehistoric finds have been found in the vicinity. It is a scheduled ancient monument no. 228970 There have been several collections of pottery found, in 1977, 1980 and 1987 Other significant finds have also included for flint artefacts from the mesolithic era, and flint tools from the neolithic era, prior to the Iron Age.

Location

The site is located at grid reference SU302753, to the southwest of the village and parish of Lambourn, in the county of Wiltshire and in part Berkshire. The site lies at a height of approximately 200m AOD. There is a public footpath that runs through the iste and bridleways to the east and south of the site. The M4 motorway lies to the immediate north and northeast. The motorway services station Membury services, and the wartime airfield, RAF Membury, also lie to the immediate north east.

Source http://en.wikipedia.org/wiki/Membury_Camp

Old Sarum

Model of Old Sarum

Old Sarum (Latin: ***Sorviodunum***) is the site of the earliest settlement of Salisbury, in England. The site contains evidence of human habitation as early as 3000 BC. Old Sarum is mentioned in some of the earliest records in the country. It is located on a hill about two miles north of modern Salisbury adjacent to the A345 road.

Old Sarum was originally an Iron age hill fort strategically placed on the conjunction of two trade routes and the River Avon. The hill fort is broadly oval in shape, 400 metres (1,300 ft) in length and 360 metres (1,180 ft) in width, it consists of a double bank and intermediate ditch with an entrance on the eastern side. The site was used by the Romans, becoming the town of *Sorviodunum*. The Saxons used the site as a stronghold against marauding Vikings, and the Normans built a stone curtain wall around the Iron age perimeter and a centrally placed castle on a motte protected by a deep dry moat. A royal palace was built within the castle for King Henry I and subsequently used by Plantagenet monarchs. A Norman cathedral and bishop's residence were built at the western end of the town.

In 1219, the cathedral was demolished in favour of the new one built near the river and the townspeople moved down to the new city, then called New Salisbury or New Sarum. The castle fell out of use and was sold for materials by King Henry VIII.

By the 19th century, the settlement was officially uninhabited and yet still had formal parliamentary representation, making it the most notorious of the rotten boroughs that existed before the Reform Act 1832.

It is now an English Heritage property and open to the public.

Early history

The Norman ditch surrounding the inner bailey

Archaeological remains of rough stone tools suggest people have occupied the hilltop area of Old Sarum since Neolithic times (around 3000 BC). There is evidence that early hunters and, later, farming communities occupied the site. A protective hill fort was constructed by the local inhabitants during the British Iron Age (around 500 BC) by creating enormous banks and ditches surrounding the hill. Numerous other hillforts of the same period can be found locally, including Figsbury Ring to the east and Vespasian's Camp to the north. The archaeologist Sir R.C. Hoare described it as "a city of high note in the remotest periods by the several barrows near it, and its proximity to the two largest stone circles in England, namely, Stonehenge and Avebury."

In the Roman occupation of Britain between AD 43 and AD 410 the site was a military station, strategically placed near the convergence of five important roads. The hill fort was marked on Roman roadmaps by the name of *Sorviodunum*. The name is believed to be derived from the Celtic language name for 'the fortress by a gentle river'. In the *Chronicle of the Britons*, the place is referred to as *Caer Gradawc*.

Cynric, King of Wessex, captured the hill in 552. The Anglo-Saxons called it *Searobyrig* and under them it ranked among the most considerable towns of the West Kingdom, gaining ecclesiastical establishments soon after the conversion of the Saxons to Christianity. In the early part of the ninth century, it was a frequent residence of Egbert of Wessex, and, in 960, King Edgar assembled a national council there to plan a defence against the Danes in the north.

Norman expansion

The castle motte seen from the east

Ruins of the Royal Palace

A motte and bailey castle was built in around 1069, three years after the Norman conquest, and the town was renamed. It is listed in the Domesday Book as Sarisburia, from which the names Sarum and Salisbury are derived. In 1086, William the Conqueror convened the prelates, nobles, sheriffs and knights of his dominions at Old Sarum to pay him homage. It is probable that part of the Domesday Book was also written at this time. Two other national councils were held there; one by William Rufus, in 1096, and another by Henry I in 1116.

Palace ruins

The construction of a cathedral and bishop's palace occurred between 1075 and 1092, during the time of Bishop Osmund. However, only five days after the cathedral was consecrated, a storm destroyed the tower roof. The final completion of the cathedral was left to the third bishop of Old Sarum, Roger of Salisbury, chancellor to King Henry I. He also oversaw the construction, between 1130–1139, of a stone Royal Palace on the castle motte.

A contemporary observer, Peter of Blois (c.1135–1203) described Old Sarum as "barren, dry, and solitary, exposed to the rage of the wind; and the church (stands) as a captive on the hill where it was built, like the ark of God shut up in the profane house of Baal." Henry II of England held his wife, Eleanor of Aquitaine, prisoner at Old Sarum.

Decline

By 1219, the limitations of space on the hilltop site had become cause for concern, with the cathedral and castle in close proximity and their respective chiefs in regular conflict. When Bishop

Remains of the former royal palace.

Altar inside the ruined chapel of the Royal Palace

Poore's men were held out of the hillfort by the King's men, Poore formally requested the cathedral's relocation.

The site of a new cathedral was consecrated later that year, and in 1220 the bishop started construction on the banks of the Avon. A new settlement grew up around it, called New Salisbury or New Sarum — eventually just known as Salisbury. By 1217, the inhabitants of Old Sarum had removed their residence, and constructed their new habitations with the materials they razed from their old. As one city increased in population and extent, so the other almost as rapidly decayed.

From the reign of Edward II in the 14th century, the borough of Old Sarum elected two members to the House of Commons, despite the fact that from at least the 17th century it had no resident voters at all. One of the members in the 18th century was William Pitt the Elder. In 1831 it had eleven voters, all of whom were landowners who lived elsewhere. This made Old Sarum the most notorious of the rotten boroughs. The Reform Act 1832 completely disfranchised Old Sarum.

Source http://en.wikipedia.org/wiki/Old_Sarum

Ringsbury Camp

Ringsbury Camp

Shown within Wiltshire

Alternate name	The Roman Camp
Location	Purton, Wiltshire
Region	South West England
Coordinates	
Area	8 acres
History	
Periods	Iron Age
Site notes	
Public access	yes, via rights of way

Ringsbury Camp is an Iron Age hill fort, thought to date from approximately the year 50BC. It is located in the civil parish of Purton in Wiltshire.

Structure

Ringsbury is a multivallate fort as it has a double-banked structure. In all about 8 acres (32,000 m) are enclosed by the surrounding walls. The fort sits at the brow of a hill with excellent views of the surrounding areas, particularly to the south, west and north. There is less of an incline towards the east. It is believed that to ensure visibility was not impeded the builders cleared all areas, but certainly the land towards the west, from trees. The banks are made from limestone rubble . These are not local rocks, thus suggesting building material was transported to the camp from further afield. The stones from the banks are very light, and are known as 'blood stones'. A reason for the lightness of the rocks was apparently due to blood soaking into the stones when they were used as missiles during battles; however, nowadays chemical weathering - carbonation - of the limestone is thought to account for their light mass.

History

Historians have suggested that the fort may not have been used continually, but as an enclosure in times of unrest. Unrest was common in these times: the fort is situated on the boundary of two old British kingdoms; and there were two major Celtic invasions in the years around which the fort was constructed. The fort is also not part of the larger chain of hill forts along the Ridgeway, such as Barbury Castle, maybe suggesting Ringsbury was an 'outpost'. There are signs of earlier habitation of the site: Neolithic flint tools have been found in the area.

Today

Several rights of way make the fort accessible. Ringsbury Camp can be reached most easily by walking west through fields from Battlewell and Restrop Road in Purton. The site has a grid reference of SU 075 867. One Iron Age coin was discovered at the camp, and is currently displayed in Purton Museum. Some local people refer to Ringsbury as 'The Roman Camp', although this does not reflect its earlier Iron Age heritage. Today Ringsbury is in grassland pasture, with the southern and western banks wooded. The centre of the camp, at one time, was ploughed, which may have destroyed any further artefacts waiting to be unearthed. Ringsbury Camp is part of Restrop Farm, a biological Site of Special Scientific Interest.

Source http://en.wikipedia.org/wiki/Ringsbury_Camp

Scratchbury Camp

Scratchbury Camp, as viewed from Battlesbury Hill

Shown within Wiltshire

Location	Wiltshire
Region	Southern England
Coordinates	
Type	Univallate hillfort
Area	37 acres (15 ha)
History	
Material	Chalk
Periods	Bronze Age, Iron Age
Associated with	Belgae
Site notes	
Excavation dates	1810, 1930, 1957
Archaeologists	E.C.Curwen
	W.F.Grimes
	William Cunnington
	Sir Richard Colt Hoare
Condition	good
Public access	footpaths

Scratchbury Camp is the site of an Iron Age univallate hillfort located on Scratchbury Hill, near the village and civil parish of Norton Bavant in Wiltshire. The fort covers an area of 37 acres (15 ha) and occupies the summit of the hill on the edge of Salisbury Plain, with its four-sided shape largely following the natural contours of the hill.

The Iron Age hillfort dates to around 100 BC, but contains the remains of an earlier and smaller D-shaped enclosure or camp. The age of this earlier earthwork is currently subject to debate, and has been variously interpreted due to the inconclusive and incomplete nature of previous and differing excavation records; it may be early Iron Age dating to around 250 BC, but it has also been interpreted as being Bronze Age, dating to around 2000 BC.

There are seven Tumuli located within the enclosure of the fort, which were excavated in the 19th Century by Sir Richard Colt Hoare and William Cunnington. Finds from excavations at that time included for relics of bone, pottery, flint, brass, and amber jewellery, most of which can be seen today at the Wiltshire Heritage Museum in Devizes. In addition other items of interest have been found in and around the site including Roman artefacts and neolithic flint and jade axe heads.

The site is listed on Wiltshire Council's Sites and Monuments Record number ST94SW200, and is also a scheduled monument number SM10213. The hillfort falls within a biological Site of Special Scientific Interest, designated as *Scratchbury & Cotley Hills SSSI*, which encompasses a total of 53.5 hectares (132 acres), being first SSSI notified in 1951.

Etymology

The name of the hill is likely to be derived from the words *scratch*, an old West Country word for the Devil; and *bury*, from the Old English word *beorg*, meaning a mound or hill, or sometimes a defense; although it could also be derived from *burh*, meaning a fortified town or a defended site.

Background

Hill forts developed in the Late Bronze and Early Iron Age, roughly the start of the first millennium BC. The reason for their emergence in Britain, and their purpose, has been a subject of debate. It has been argued that they could have been military sites constructed in response to invasion from continental Europe, sites built by invaders, or a military reaction to social tensions caused by an increasing population and consequent pressure on agriculture. The dominant view since the 1960s has been that the increasing use of iron led to social changes in Britain. Deposits of iron ore were located in different places to the tin and copper ore necessary to make bronze, and as a result trading patterns shifted and the old elites lost their economic and social status. Power passed into the hands of a new group of people. Archaeologist Barry Cunliffe believes that population increase still played a role and has stated "[the forts] provided defensive possibilities for the community at those times when the stress [of an increasing population] burst out into open warfare. But I wouldn't see them as having been built because there was a state of war. They would be functional as defensive strongholds when there were tensions and undoubtedly some of them were attacked and destroyed, but this was not the only, or even the most significant, factor in their construction".

Description

Iron Age Hillfort

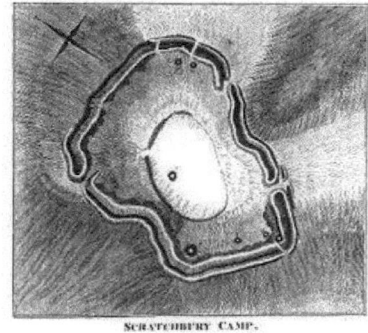

Pencil sketch of Scratchbury camp by Sir Richard Colt-Hoare, 1810, *The Ancient History of Wiltshire*, Vol.i, p.70

The steeply contoured sides of Scratchbury Hill form natural defenses to the north, west and southwestern sides, and in part to a small area of the eastern flank. Elsewhere on the hill the contours are less steep and afford easier access, with the southeastern boundary merging into the adjacent Cotley Hill with only a small change in level. The Iron Age fortifications at Scratchbury Camp comprise of a single large ditch and rampart to the most steeply contoured flanks, with some secondary counterscarps to the more accessible sides. The fort, as measured from the ramparts, has a circumfrence of 1,846 yd (1,688 m)

The inner earthworks are typical of a "quarry-ditch" formation, whereby the material excavated from the inner ditch is used to create the rampart. The fortifications are best preserved on the western side of the hill where the ditch is between 5 and 8 metres (16 and 26 ft) wide and up to 1 metre (3.3 ft) deep. The banks and ditches are generally uneven in height and depth, which is thought to be evidence for a 'gang dug' construction of the earthworks. Elsewhere, the enclosure is defined by a bank 3 to 6 metres (9.8 to 20 ft) in height above the ditch bottom, the ditch being 4 to 6 metres (13 to 20 ft) wide and up to 0.5 metres (1.6 ft) deep. On parts of the eastern side of the fort the ditch is absent and is replaced by a ledge of between 3 to 8 metres (9.8 to 26 ft) wide. There are two original entrances to the fort on the eastern side, and a possible third on the northwest side.

Much of the north and west areas of the interior appear to have been densely settled, as demonstrated by the traces of approximately 100 probable structures. These survive mainly as shallow circular hollows of between 5 to 10 metres (16 to 33 ft) in diameter and up to 0.6 metres (2.0 ft) deep. The best preserved is a rectangular platform immediately within the southern terminal of the western entrance. The location and unusual morphology suggests a special function for this structure, and it is perhaps plausible that a 'guard chamber' or sentry was positioned here.

Earlier Enclosure

Within the centre of the hillfort lies the remains of an earlier and smaller D-shaped inner earthwork enclosure of circa 3.5 hectares (8.6 acres), and excavated by E.C.Curwen in 1930. Today, all that really remains of this enclosure is one well defined lynchet of approximately 0.5 metres (1.6 ft) high along the southern section. This feature bears a resemblance to a similar such enclo-

Detail of the northeast flank earthwork defenses at Scratchbury Camp

sure at Yarnbury Castle, and was originally interpreted by Curwen to be a Neolithic causewayed enclosure due to its interrupted nature, and the discovery at the site of jade and flint axes.

Subsequent excavations by W.F. Grimes in 1957 re-interpreted this feature to be an earlier Iron Age enclosure dating to approximately 250 BC, with Iron Age pottery found within the primary fill. It was therefore speculated that the visible interruptions have been made by post Medieval ploughing. Faint traces of a remnant bank survive along the north and west sections, and an adjoining ditch has a causewayed nature, and survives in short segments varying between 30 to 50 metres (98 to 160 ft) in length. There is also evidence of a single original west facing entrance currently discernable as a 15 metres (49 ft) wide gap in the enclosure boundary. The straight southeastern side of the enclosure is formed by a ditch that is truncated by the main hillfort boundary, and this again has been interpreted as further evidence that the linear ditch and contiguous enclosure pre-date the main hillfort.

However, more recent aerial and photographic surveys have meant that W. F.Grimes' re-interpretation may have been in error. A detailed survey undertaken between 1994 and 1995 by the field survey teams of the Royal Commission on the Historical Monuments of England have suggested that the feature is in fact more likely to be a Neolithic causewayed enclosure as originally interpreted by E.C.Curwen. One possible explanation for the apparent confusion in dating this feature is that Grimes may not have excavated fully to the primary fill. The surveys suggest that the feature clearly has causeways, and low winter sun photography shows that the enclosure continues beyond what was previously believed to be its eastern edge, to form a sub-circular rather than D-shaped enclosure feature. The 'crop mark visible on aerial photographs shows a continuation of the curve to the southeast of the straight side, thus roughly completing a circle. It should be noted that this feature has also been interpreted as a possible base for a palisaded enclosure. There is also a probable link between the likely neolithic causewayed enclosure and the surrounding barrow cemetery, which would have followed later.

Panoramic view of Scratchbury Hill, as viewed from the northwest. The hillfort earthworks are clearly visible crowning the hill.

Later Features

There is also a Romano-British or later ditch, running east to west, which turns south sharply at the southwest corner of the hillfort, and which partly overlies the earlier Iron Age earthworks. The main ramparts appear to have been built in the 1st century BC.

Construction Phases

The archaeological evidence suggests that Scratchbury Camp was built in at least two but perhaps three phases. The 1st phase is the defined by the curvilinear portion of the interior 'D'-shaped enclosure.

Whether there were distinct 2nd and 3rd Iron Age phases, or merely a re-alignment in the 2nd phase is unclear. The scarp subdividing the early fort is a possible indication of a 2nd phase, but may have been the setting out for a bank that was never utilised. In its 3rd and final phase it seems possible that the fort, having been 'laid out' to include the large barrow, was then further extended to encompass the whole of the

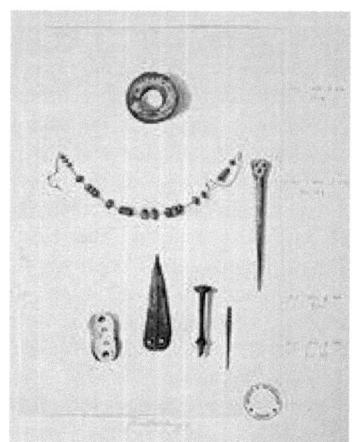

Drawing of finds from the Scratchbury Grave Group, 1869; William Pilsbury after Richard Colt-Hoare (1758–1838); Watercolour on paper, 26.7 x 17.8 (cm); located at the Society of Antiquaries of London

top of the hill in order to make full defensive use of the natural slopes and resulting in the present day configuration.

Archaeology

Excavations at the site have revealed many items from Neolithic, Bronze Age, Iron Age and Romano British periods. Most of the various finds discovered are now preserved at the Wiltshire Heritage Museum in Devizes.

Most recently Professor William Francis Grimes partially excavated the inner earthworks on the site in the 1950s. Finds included for Iron Age pottery. In 1880 two Bronze Age axes were found at the site. A Roman bronze spoon was found on the site in 1804.

Sir Richard Colt Hoare also records the discoveries of a neolithic jade axe and a ground flint axe with 'British and Roman' pottery inside the camp, as excavated by William Cunnington in 1802. The flint axe is of polished white flint, with the end re-chipped, and was found at the entrance to Scratchbury Camp. It measures 86 mm (3.4 in) long, by 63 mm (2.5 in) wide, and 25 mm (0.98 in) high.

The hillfort also contains seven tumuli within its boundaries, which were excavated between 1802 and 1804 by Sir Richard Colt Hoare and William Cunnington. However, as the three-age system had not yet been introduced, they were unable to date their finds and therefore at a disadvantage when trying to interpret them. The tumuli were re-recorded in the 1957 surveys by W.F. Grimes. Full details and descriptions from the reports and writings of Sir Richard Colt-Hoare, and William Cunnington are given in the table below:

Wiltshire Heritage Museum ref name	R. Colt-Hoare ref no.	Type	Diameter	He
Norton Bavant Tumuli G1	1	Bowl Barrow	81 ft (25 m)	3 f 91
Norton Bavant Tumuli G2	2	Bowl barrow	45 ft (14 m)	3.5 1 n
Norton Bavant Tumuli G3	3	Bowl barrow	36 ft (11 m)	2 f 61
Norton Bavant Tumuli G4	7	Bowl barrow	100 ft (30 m)	10 0 n

Norton Bavant Tumuli G4a	6	Bowl barrow	unknown	unl
Norton Bavant Tumuli G4b	4	Bowl barrow	15 ft (4.6 m)	0.2 (0. 07(
Norton Bavant Tumuli G4c	5	Bowl barrow	30 ft (9.1 m)	1.5 46

There are several other tumuli located on the adjacent and co-joined Cotley Hill, on the crown of that hill itself is a further Bronze Age tumuli surrounded by an Iron Age enclosure.

Geography

1817 Ordnance Survey Map of Scratchbury Camp

Scratchbury is located on the edge of the chalk plateau of Salisbury Plain, and within the area of **Norton Bavant Chalk Downland Edge**, as described by the *West Wiltshire Landscape Character Assessment*. Forming part of a system of chalk downlands throughout eastern and southern England formed by the rocks of the Chalk Group, the landscape is underlain by a combination of Lower, Middle and Upper Chalk supporting shallow well drained calcareous silty soils over chalk on slopes and crests. Typically these landscapes may be described as 'dramatic', due to their local scale, visual aesthetic and undulating nature. Escarpments are often formed where layers of chalk have been compressed to form a fold, or where the chalk has been faulted, resulting in accelerated erosion along the line of the weakness.

For the Norton Bavant Chalk Downland Edge, the 'character' of this area encompasses three distinctive, steeply sloping hills (Middle Hill, Scratchbury Hill, and Cotley Hill), which form a distinct and somewhat isolated unit of Chalk Downland Edge. The hills are covered with long fields, which are predominantly arable, with occasional patches of rough remnant chalk grassland and scrub situated on the top of the hills. Many chalk grassland slopes in England show the mark of centuries of grazing by sheep, the slopes bearing a stepped or striped appearance formed by a mixture of soil creep and sheep paths, and such erosion is visible on the slopes of Scratchbury Hill. Regular patches and belts of mixed woodland populate parts of the lower slopes. Imber range perimeter paths run across the top of the hills, providing public access to the area.

Ecology

Scratchbury Camp as viewed from the southwest: the distinctive features of Scratchbury Hill, including the ramparts of the hill fort and one of the taller barrows, are clearly defined

Scratchbury is located in an area of unimproved grassland on the edge of Salisbury Plain, which is the largest remaining area of calcareous grassland in north-west Europe. The local area supports a rich and diverse grassland flora and an important associated butterfly fauna, which led to it being declared a biological Site of Special Scientific Interest in 1951. Designated as *Scratchbury & Cotley Hills SSSI*, the site encompasses a total of 53.5 hectares (132 acres).

The grassland generally is dominated by Sheep's Fescue *Festuca ovina*, Red Fescue *Festuca rubra* and Upright Brome *Bromus erectus*. There are also several varieties of herbs characteristic to the Wiltshire downland, including for Devil's Bit Scabious *Succisa pratensis*, Saw-wort *Serratula tinctoria* and Chalk Milkwort *Polygala calcarea* There are also many other native and site specific plants, including for orchids, meadow grasses, nettles, and other flora.

Within the hillfort, a richer, more mesotrophic grassland is present, most probably reflecting past agricultural use and improvement. There are also small areas of Hawthorn *Crataegus monogyna*, and Elder *Sambucus* scrub, particularly along the lower slopes of the downland and on the earthworks. These provide valuable shelter for invertebrates on an otherwise open and exposed site.

The Adonis Blue Butterfly can be found on and around Scratchbury Camp

The site is of high entomological interest, with 29 varieties of resident breeding species of butterfly recorded. The horseshoe vetch *Hippocrepis comosa* is locally plentiful and supports both the Chalkhill Blue *Lysandra coridon* and the Adonis Blue *Lysandra bellargus* butterflies. Other butterfly species to be found on and around the site include for the Duke of Burgundy *Hamaeris lucina*, the Grizzled Skipper *Pyrgus malvae*, the Dark Green Fritillary *Argynnis aglaja* and the Small Blue *Cupido minimus*.

Other insect groups on the site are less well surveyed, but several rare species have been noted, including for six species of weevil *Curculionoidea*, eight species of plant bugs, *Hemiptera* and *Homoptera*; and two species of Chrysomelid beetle, *Apthona herbigrada* and *Mantura matthewsii*, both of which feed on the rock rose *Helianthemum*. Day flying moths recorded include for the Wood Tiger *Parasemia plantaginis* and the rare Forester Moth *Adscita globulariae*.

Poetry

Siegfried Sassoon

The English poet and author Siegfried Sassoon, (1886–1967), who lived nearby at Heytesbury House, wrote about Scratchbury Camp, subtly capturing the ambience of the Wiltshire Downs on a summers day, whilst touching on the pervasive military presence of that age and the historical timelessness of the area:

Along the grave green downs, this idle afternoon,
shadows of loitering silver clouds, becalmed in blue,
bring, like unfoldment of a flower, the best of June.

Shadows outspread in spacious movement, always you
have dappled the downs and valleys at this time of year,
while larks, ascending shrill, praised freedom as they flew.

Now, through that song, a fighter squadron's drone I hear
from Scratchbury Camp, whose turfed and cowslip'd rampart seems
more hill than history, ageless and oblivion-blurred.

I walk the fosse, once manned by bronze and flint head spear;
on war's imperious wing the shafted sun ray gleams:
one with the warm sweet air of summer stoops the bird.

Cloud shadows, drifting slow like heedless daylight dreams,
dwell and dissolve; uncircumstanced they pause and pass.
I watch them go. My horse, contented, crops the grass.

—Siegfried Sassoon, *On Scratchbury Camp, 1942, from Collected Poems 1908–1956.*

Location

The site is located at grid reference ST912442, to the east of the town of Warminster, and to the north of the village and civil parish of Norton Bavant, in the county of Wiltshire. The hill has a summit of 197 m (646 ft) AOD. Nearby to the northwest lies *Middle Hill*, and further northwest the hillfort of Battlesbury Camp, on *Battlesbury Hill*. To the southeast lies *Cotley Hill*. The site and surrounding downs are easily accessible by public footpath, the Wessex Ridgeway and the *Imber Range perimeter path* follow the northern ramparts of the fort, however care must be taken not to stray into the Military Firing ranges of Salisbury Plain immediately to the northeast. Cranborne Chase and West Wiltshire Downs Area of Outstanding Natural Beauty lies to the south.

Source http://en.wikipedia.org/wiki/Scratchbury_Camp

Sidbury Hill, Wiltshire

Sidbury Hill

Sidbury Hill

Shown within Wiltshire

Location	Wiltshire
Coordinates	
Area	17 acres (7 ha)
History	
Periods	Iron Age
Site notes	
Public access	not easy

Sidbury Hill, or **Sidbury Camp**, is the site of an Iron Age bivallate hillfort located in Wiltshire. The site is sub-triangular in shape, and approximately 17 acres in area, and is constructed on the site of a neolithic settlement. The hill offers excellent defensive slopes on all sides, which have been supplemented by the double ditch and rampart earthworks. The settlement and hillfort were partially excavated in the 19th century and the 1950s. There were finds of pottery and other artefacts. A straight, well defined ditch extends from the main entrance on the northwest side. This earthwork is one element in an extensive system of boundaries founded on and around Sidbury Hill. The southern section is straight and well preserved. A neolithic settlement site was discovered during the excavation in the 1950s, being of a section of the south-east rampart of the hill fort. A number of flint flakes and tools were recovered.

The site is a scheduled national monument no.10064. The site was wooded, but the trees planted in the 1960s are now being removed, (since Sept 2002) and the area is being allowed to revert to the natural chalk downland. Access to the site is difficult as it is on, or near, Ministry of Defence land, and there are many tank tracks and occasional artillery firing in the area. There are also numerous ditches, barrows, trackways, field systems, and tumuli in the area.

Location

The site is located at grid reference SU216505, to the northwest of the small town of Tidworth, in the county of Wiltshire. The hill has a summit of 223-mACD. There are public footpaths and bridleways in the area, however the surrounding land is managed by the MOD and access to the hill fort may be restricted at times.

Source http://en.wikipedia.org.wiki/Sidbury_Hill,_Wiltshire

Vespasian's Camp

Stonehenge, Avebury and Associated Sites
Name as inscribed on the World Heritage List

Northwestern inner bank of Vespasian's Camp

Country	United Kingdom of Great Britain and Northern Ireland
Type	Cultural
Criteria	i, ii, iii
Reference	373
UNESCO region	Europe and North America
Inscription history	
Inscription	1986 (10th Session)

Vespasian's Camp is an Iron Age Hillfort in the town of Amesbury, Wiltshire, England. It is located less than 2 miles from the Neolithic and Bronze Age site of Stonehenge and was built on a hill next to the Stonehenge Avenue.

Etymology

Although the Roman general Vespasian campaigned through Wessex after the Roman invasion of Britain, there is no evidence to suggest he came to this hillfort or had any military base here. The name was given to the site by William Camden, who during the Elizabethan era toured the area and gave the hill its romanticised name.

Context

The hillfort stands on the western fringe of Amesbury and borders the River Avon on its southern side, and the A303 on its northern edge. It is inside the boundaries of the Stonehenge World Heritage Site inscribed in 1986. Several other hill-forts are located nearby, including Danebury to the east, Sidbury Hill and Casterley Camp to the north, Yarnbury Castle to the west, and Figsbury Ring and Old Sarum to the south. Ogbury Camp 3 miles south may have been a satellite enclosure of Vespasian's Camp. From north to south the hill-fort is 730m in overall length and 374m wide at the southern end, narrowing to 100m wide at the northern end. It encloses an area of some 15 hectares. The bank is up to 40m wide and up to 6 metres high above the ditch bottom. The ditch is up to 10m wide with a low counterscarp bank up to 18m wide on the outside of the ditch, creating a maximum overall width of the hill-fort's defences of 68m.

Prehistory of the site

The hill on which Vespasian's Camp stands was used during the Neolithic era, as indicated by the Neolithic pits found near the centre. Excavations suggest that the hill may have been part of the Stonehenge ritual landscape during this period. The first building of the hillforts banks is believed to have occurred during the late Bronze Age (between 1100BC-800BC) with some later building in the early Iron Age (700BC-350BC). There appears to be an entrance on the northern and southern sides. Unlike most regular hillforts of the time, Vespasian's Camp has a somewhat unusual shape, appearing from above as an arrowhead. The southern banks are constructed with angled corners (possibly to take the shape of the hill alongside the Avon into account), which is not a common feature in most round hillforts in the south.

Excavations have revealed a metre thick layer of domestic waste that suggests the hill was heavily occupied after the banks were constructed. The absence of significant middle Iron Age finds suggests that the population on the hill had declined by then.

It had been assumed that most of the archaeology had been lost during the 18th century landscaping by a Marquess of Queensberry but documentary research showed that the hillfort had escaped most of the landscaping and excavations were begun in 2005. These focused on an area near Vespasian's Camp known as Blick Mead. The first finds discovered tools ranging as far back as the mesolithic. It also revealed that what had been thought to be a water feature was an ancient spring which might have been part of a seasonal lake.

Further work in 2010 uncovered a 12cm layer of mesolithic material including 10,000 pieces of struck flint and over 300 pieces of animal bone, a find described by Professor Tim Darvill as "the most important discovery at Stonehenge in many years." The struck flint tools were discovered in pristine condition, sharp enough to cut the fingers of some of the excavators, and it is believe that the layer may extend a few hundred metres more. One tool was made cut of worked slate. The possible sources of the slate are either slate glacial erratics (not known to exist in the area or North Wales. If this is the source it shows that thousands of years before Stonehenge this may have been a "special place to gather".

Evidence suggests that the spring area was used for huge feasts including the consumption of aurochs and as a centre for tool making. In addition an unusual form of Mesolithic domestic site was found, a semi-permanent site for families called a 'homebase'. Dates for the site show that is was used between 6250 and 4700 BC making it the oldest residential site in this area.

The Middle Ages until today

A road came to be constructed over the hilltop in the middle ages, and now separates the southern corner from the rest of the fort. The A303 was cut through the northern section of the hill in the 1970s, just below the northernmost bank.

During the 18th Century the hillfort was landscaped as part of the Marquis of Queensbury's grounds around Amesbury Abbey. A grotto, vista and paths were constructed and substantial tree planting was carried out.

Source http://en.wikipedia.org/wiki/Vespasian's_Camp

Whitesheet Hill

Whitesheet Hill

Elevation	245 m (804 ft)
Location	
Location	Wiltshire, England
OS grid	ST803346
Topo map	OS *Landranger*
Climbing	
Easiest route	Public footpaths and bridleways

Whitesheet Hill is a 136.1 hectare biological Site of Special Scientific Interest in Wiltshire, notified in 1965. As one of the most westerly areas of downland in Britain the area is noted for its chalky farmland which contains a rich variety of rare and protected fauna and flora. The hill is also the site of a neolithic causeway camp and barrows; and an Iron Age hill fort. The Roman road which runs along the hill was at one time the main route through the Selwood Forest. The hill is part of the Stourhead estate and has been in the ownership of the National Trust since 1946.

Whitesheet hill is located at White Sheet Down, in the parish of Kilmington near the small town of Mere on the A303 in West Wiltshire, England. It is situated within the Cranborne Chase and West Wiltshire Downs Area of Outstanding Natural Beauty, and has extensive views over Somerset, Dorset and Wiltshire. It is home to White Sheet Radio Flying Club who use it as a slope soaring site for fun and competition flying.

Prehistoric archaeology

There are some 12 ancient burial mounds (barrows) on the hill dating from 1800 BC.

The site was excavated by Sir Richard Hoare, 2nd Baronet in the early 19th century:
Immediately on ascending the hill called Whitesheet, we find ourselves surrounded by British antiquities. The road intersects an ancient earthen work, of a circular form, and which, from the slightness of its vallum, appears to have been of high antiquity. Adjoining it is a large barrow, which we opened in October 1807, and found it had contained a skeleton, and had been investigated before.
On a point of land near this barrow are three others, all of which, by the defaced appearance of their summits, seemed to have attracted the notice of former antiquaries. No 1, the nearest to the edge of the hill, had certainly been opened, and appears to have contained a double interment. The primary one was an interment of burned bones deposited within a shallow cist, in an urn rudely formed, and badly baked. Above it was a skeleton with its head laid towards the south, and which from its position and perfect preservation appears not to have been disturbed. Its mouth was wide open, and it "grinn'd horribly a ghastly smile," a singularity we have never before met with.

p42, "Ancient History of Wiltshire" v2, 1812

Source http://en.wikipedia.org/wiki/Whitesheet_Hill

Yarnbury Castle

Yarnbury Castle

The earthwork ramparts and ditches of Yarnbury Castle

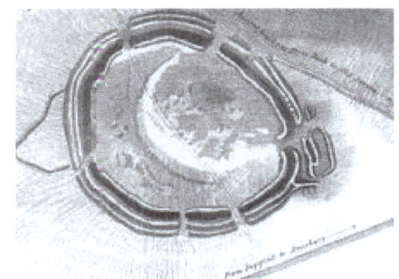

Pencil sketch of Yarnbury Castle by Sir Richard Colt-Hoare, 1810, from *The Ancient History of Wiltshire*

Shown within Wiltshire

Location	Wiltshire
Region	Southern England
Coordinates	
Type	hillfort
Area	28.5 acres (11.5 ha)
Height	167 m (548 ft)
History	
Material	Chalk
Founded	Iron age
Site notes	
Excavation dates	1932, 1987
Archaeologists	Mrs.M.E.Cunnington RCHME
Public access	no

Yarnbury Castle is the site of a multi-phase, multivallate iron age hillfort near the village and civil parish of Steeple Langford, in Wiltshire. The site covers an area of 28.5 acres (11.5 ha), and has been extensively surveyed and investigated by the Royal Commission on the Historical Monuments of England (RCHME) in 1991, with finds of iron age and Romano-British pottery, iron age and roman coins, and burials of human remains. There is much evidence of prolonged and extensive settlement of the site including for the evidence of around 130 separate structures of various sizes, most probably representing a mix of round houses, pits, and other features.

The earthworks of Yarnbury Castle are also a biological Site of Special Scientific Interest(SSSI) first notified in 1951.

Archaeology

The earthworks at Yarnbury comprise of three ramparts with outer ditches. The outer ramparts measure up to 3.5 m (11 ft) high, and the ditches a further 1.7 m (5.6 ft) deep, and are encroached upon by the centre rampart in places, suggesting that the inner and centre rampart are a later feature. The overall width of the earthworks is generally uniform at around 17 m (56 ft). The earthworks are generally well preserved, except in the northeastern side where the outermost ditch has been lost due to the encroachment of a downland driveway. In the centre of the hillfort lies an earlier and smaller single banked enclosure of 5.2 ha (13 acres) in area, and with an entrance in the western side of the earthwork.

The main earthworks are thought to date from around 100 BC, with the earlier inner circuit being from about 300 BC, according to pottery finds from early iron age through to Romano-British, including for Samian of around 160 AD. The main entrance to the hillfort lies on the eastern side of the site, with a complex of earthwork fortifications. There is a further entrance at the northern end, possibly a later addition, with the entrance to the western side thought to be non-original or later so serve a smaller sub-rectangular Romano-British enclosure on that side of the fort.

Within the fort there is much evidence for many structures, mainly circular in plan, and within compounds with low earth banks. The structures vary between 7 m (23 ft) and 15 m (49 ft) in diameter, and up to 1.0 m (3.3 ft) deep. In particular, in the north and east of the site, and between the earlier enclosure and the inner rampart, there are a number of large compounds containing structures clearly visible, many with evidence for possible stone footings. It is also evident that a number of them overlap and indicate a prolonged and varied occupation of the site.

There have been numerous inhumations found at the site including for two within pits, and other isolated human bones found in other pits. Also nine complete or partial remains of newly born and young infants have been found in the bottom of the earthwork ditches. Archaeological finds include for pottery sherds, flint flakes, iron slag, Celtic coins, and bronze brooches. From later periods finds also include for much Roman items, such as pottery, tiles, coins and three burials in graves.

Sheep fairs

The Winterbourne Stoke sheep fair was held on the site from the 18th century until 1916, when the area was commandeered by the army. There are several prominent features associated with this former use, including for several sheep folds to the south eastern corner of the hillfort. These are grouped in two blocks of 8, with low mounded earthworks clearly visible and covering an area of 120 m (390 ft) by 90 m (300 ft). They do not however appear in Sir Richard Colt Hoares pencil sketch of the site from 1810, indicating that these date from later in the 19th century

The local author Ella Noyes (1863-1949) from Sutton Very wrote in her book *Salisbury Plain* (1913), the following about the event:

Once a year Yarnbury becomes reanimate on the day of the Horse and Sheep Fair, October 4th, held in this lonely trysting place by immemorial tradition. Here.. the flocks..stand close packed in pens; bunches of young ponies are tied up in one corner.. and near by are the sober cart-horses, their plaited manes and tails aprick with ornaments of straw. The vendor of sheep bells spreads his metal wares upon the ground.. the purchase of sheep bells is a serious matter, good ones costing as much as five shillings..In the good old days, up to within the memory of people still living, the fair was followed by horse races next day, and sports of all kinds. But now the pleasure part of the meeting has been abandoned; the folk disperse quietly soon after noon, when business is done, leaving Yarnbury to the silent occupation of its prehistoric ghosts for another year.

Ecology

The marsh fritillary can be found at Yarnbury Castle

Yarnbury Castle is located in an area of unimproved grassland on the upper chalk north of the Wylye Valley, and on the edge of Salisbury Plain, which is the largest remaining area of calcareous grassland in north-west Europe. The local area supports a rich and diverse grassland flora, which led to it being declared a biological Site of Special Scientific Interest in 1951. Designated as *Yarnbury Castle SSSI*, the site encompasses a total of 9.1 hectares (22 acres).

The SSSI designation for the site arises due to interest in the biodiversity and species present upon the earthworks of the fort themselves, with the inner and surrounding parts of the site being of improved agricultural grassland of little interest. The earthworks support a rich chalk grassland flora, including for several rare species. There are 16 species of grass and sedge recorded; with upright brome *Bromus erectus*, sheep's fescue *Festuca ovina*, quaking grass *Briza media*, crested hair-grass *Koeleria cristata*, and dwarf sedge *Carex humilis*. Various herb species include for dwarf thistle *Cirsium acaule*, chalk milkwort *Polygala calcarea*, horseshoe vetch *Hippocrepis comosa*, common thyme *Thymus praecox*, squinancywort *Asperula cynanchica* and common rock-rose *Helianthemum nummularium*.

Rarer national species include for field fleawort *Senecio integrifolius*, bastard-toadflax *Thesium humifusum*, and burnt orchid *Orchis usulata*, Fragrant orchid *Gymnadenia conopsea*, and other orchids.

The site was previously populated with scattered juniper *Juniperus communis* bushes, but these are now removed and the current grazing regime ensures that they do not return. There are some invertebrates recorded, including for marsh fritillary *Eurodryas aurinia* and small heath *Coenonympha pamphilus* butterflys, and a number of downland birds are present including for the skylark, corn bunting and grey partridge.

Source http://en.wikipedia.org/wiki/Yarnbury_Castle